Speak
Peace

Words of Wisdom, Work, & Wonder

Speak
Peace

Words of Wisdom, Work, & Wonder

Compiled by

Lyn Ford &
Sherry Norfolk

Parkhurst Brothers Publishers
MARION, MICHIGAN

www.parkhurstbrothers.com

Consumers may order Parkhurst Brothers books from their favorite online or bricks-and-mortar booksellers, expecting prompt delivery. Parkhurst Brothers books are distributed to the trade through the Chicago Distribution Center. Trade and library orders may be placed through Ingram Book Company, Baker & Taylor, Follett Library Resources and other book industry wholesalers. To order from Chicago Distribution Center, phone 1-800-621-2736 or fax to 800-621-8476. Copies of this and other Parkhurst Brothers Publishers titles are available to organizations and corporations for purchase in quantity by contacting Special Sales Department at our home office location, listed on our web site. Manuscript submission guidelines for this publishing company are available at our web site.

Printed in the United States of America
First Edition, September 2019
Printing history: 2019   2020   2021   2022   12 11 10 9 8 7 6 5 4 3 2 1
Library of Congress Cataloging in Publication Data:
1.Title–Speak Peace: words of wisdom, work and wonder.
2. Authors: Norfolk, Sherry and Ford, Lyn
3. Subject: peace-building, education for peace and social justice
c. pm.   Original trade paperback, 2019
anthology of essays and folktales for use in peace education

ISBN: Trade Paperback   978162491-141-2
ISBN: e-book   978162491-141-5

Cover and interior design by   Linda D. Parkhurst, PhD
Proofread by   Bill and Barbara Paddack
Acquired for Parkhurst Brothers Publishers
And edited by: Ted Parkhurst

092019

Dedication

To those who offered heartfelt responses to my question
on Facebook—you will find some of your responses in the
Introduction. We asked, "What do we do?" Your wisdom, work, and
words are reflected in the quotations, articles, and stories you will
find here.

To those who will find treasures here, and ways to share
what you find.

To those who speak Peace and seek Light for the world.

To those who sacrificed for some sense of peace, for those now
living in a less-than-peaceful world.
Our children deserve a better one.

To the dedicated storytellers and listeners whose minds,
hearts and spirits tirelessly
Speak Peace!

Love, courage and the blessings of shared stories to all of you.

—*Lyn Ford and Sherry Norfolk*

Contents

Foreword
Kiran Singh Sirah

I'M WRITING THIS FOREWORD ON JULY 5, 2017, a year to the day since Alton Sterling, a thirty-seven-year-old black man, was shot to death by police in Baton Rouge, Louisiana. I happened to be in Baton Rouge at the time, in town to help a friend move. The shooting occurred just about a mile from where I was staying, but I didn't hear about it until the next morning. I went to the hotel café to work on my laptop and I sensed tension in the air. Something had happened.

In the café, I sat amongst a diverse gathering of people. Some were in suits, many of whom were clearly in work meetings. Some seemed to be on vacation. Together, we stared up at the news pouring from the big screen mounted on the wall. It was a mainstream news channel—it doesn't matter which one—that was reporting on a riot in Baton Rouge. I looked around, and there was no evidence of a riot. (The hotel was downtown.) Nor did I see any evidence of rioting over the course of the rest of that day. People had gathered, but it was to pay their respects, not an act of unrest. That's called a vigil, not a riot. It's quite a normal act when a community is in shock.

Later that afternoon, I saw one young black woman standing in the intersection of a street; she held a sign that read, "We are all Alton

Sterling." I stopped to talk to her. Her name was Tam Williams, and she was a twenty-four-year-old documentary filmmaker. She told me about growing up in Baton Rouge, which she described as segregated. She let me take a photo that I used to create a Facebook post that evening. I thought it was so brave of her to stand there alone. She was compelled to do something. That night, the downtown area was eerily quiet, but my mind was not still; it seemed important to share what I had witnessed.

As it happened, Lyn Ford was posting about Alton Sterling's death, too. We're friends and colleagues. Although we haven't known one another all that long, I've come to respect her passion for teaching and building community as a storyteller, a teacher, a community-builder, a mother, and a grandmother. We set up a time to talk after I'd returned home, and it was then that she told me about wanting to do something in response. Like that woman in the intersection, she felt compelled to do something. This book is the result.

Both Lyn and her friend and co-author, Sherry Norfolk, are well-established writers, workshop presenters, and teaching artists. But as the president of the International Storytelling Center (ISC), I know them best in their capacity as storytellers. I met them both within weeks after I had taken my position at ISC in 2013. We were all at the National Storytelling Network conference in Richmond, Virginia—my first dive into meeting America's storytelling community. They stood out to me in this sea of new people, and I have since had the opportunity to see their profound commitment to using the art of storytelling as an educational tool.

Lyn is a fourth-generation storyteller and educator who has worked with ISC for many years as a performer and a workshop leader. She has even worked with me as I have developed my own stories. To this day, whatever story I'm working on, I imagine her face in front of me. I tell it as if I were telling it to her. Sherry, too, has much experience as a teacher and nationally and internationally known storyteller, helping shape the quality of the writing of generations of her students. Like Lyn, and with Lyn when their schedules permit it, Sherry offers acclaimed workshops to help educators sharpen their tools.

As it happens, I started my own career as an educator, a high school art teacher. Newly qualified, I got my first placement at the tender age of twenty-two—a three-month placement in north London, teaching in a public school. I quickly came to understand that I wasn't just teaching art but helping students understand their often-confusing world, as well as their place in it. I was helping them tell their stories and build the confidence to share them with others. Teaching would become the catalyst for my pursuit of a career in the arts—a career of helping people tell their stories.

Being able to channel the feelings of isolation, marginalization, and conflict that I had felt growing into the work was powerful. As the son of refugees in a predominantly "white" English town at what was then the height of the anti-immigrant movement, I was well acquainted with feeling personally ostracized, as well as with much larger forces of social unrest. But I always drew strength from the stories of my family, as well as stories from the wider world that I was exposed to at school. These spoken stories gave me a sense of belonging and understanding. They helped me carve out a space in which I could develop my own opinion within the broader context of what I saw on the news.

This little book offers that same sense of strength-through-story. It is, in a sense, a collection of stories, offering diverse perspectives and personal experiences told in parallel to the stories we are inundated with on television and social media. Sharing stories is a powerful act, particularly in a country torn by what feels like an ever-increasing divide. It's something that people need now more than ever. As the news in Baton Rouge demonstrated to me one year ago today, we need to go deeper than the stories we're offered through the news media; we need to talk to individuals about their lived experience. Sharing our stories has the power to change minds, build bridges, and support communities.

The narratives, quotations, and articles in this book are drawn from the direct experiences of storytellers and their diverse backgrounds, as well as from their repertoires, researched collections, and recollections. They were chosen as focal points to motivate us to reflect in a way that promotes peace, incites wisdom, facilitates conflict resolution, and inspires. Lyn and Sherry—both well-connected storytelling professionals and advocates for storytelling in education and for peace—are precisely the right people to guide us along the way.

Storytellers can't resolve every deep-seated disparity or, with one story or program, bring about world peace. But they can offer us stories, both printed and spoken, drawn from a rich array of experiences and traditions that can be contemplated, read aloud, and used in classroom discussions by students, teachers, and other educators. Listening to stories that differ from our own experiences, we can begin to empathize, to understand, and to make connections in unexpected ways.

At a personal level, we can be empowered to take the initiative to bridge divides, promote awareness, and simply appreciate stories constructed to build a path toward empathy. We can also use stories to better understand who we are collectively, as a country, and as citizens of the world.

I consider this book as an intervention. It has a purpose fueled by deep need and collective desire. Its goal is to empower, to invest in *us*, to tell stories that will promote awareness on the issues that matter to us, as well as the simple goal of helping people envision a more peaceful world.

Whether you read from start to finish or dip in and out, read alone or with a group of friends, it's important to envision these vibrant possibilities even as we commemorate and honor those whose lives have been needlessly taken.

I appreciate this work from so many different angles. As president of the International Storytelling Center, I'm very much tapped into the power that stories have to change the world. As a peacebuilder, I appreciate stories that facilitate understanding. As an educator, I'm pleased to have a new, accessible resource to recommend to both students and teachers. And as a human being—someone who has witnessed and been subject to violent conflict—I feel blessed to recommend this book, which will no doubt play an integral role as we use storytelling to build a better world.

Kiran Singh Sirah
Peace Activist, Poet, Artist
President of the International Storytelling Center

"Let it Begin with Me"
Linda Schuyler Ford

Sandy Hook.

Boston.

Paris.

Orlando.

Las Vegas

Guns, bombs, riots.

Racism. Sexism. Homophobia. Bullying. Brutality by those in authority.

In this still-new century, a sense of shocked helplessness has affected all of us. For some, that emotion was followed by a call to action.

The urgent need to do something, do *something*, grew in me over the summer of 2016, when social media shared relentless reminders of the widespread anger and fear that gripped Americans and our friends around the world.

In June of 2016, I began reaching out to storytelling friends who all agreed to plan concerts and story events promoting peace. The idea spread through Facebook. September 21, the International Day of Peace, would become a day of Stories for Peace across the country.

Preparations included deep communication among the story-tellers. "Promoting peace" was not enough. The concept doesn't invite investment. We needed to do more than tell a few stories and go home. The gatherings needed to be an invitation to introspection, conversation, and true connection.

In my own house concert, folktales, personal stories, and poems were told. Our emcee, Saundra Kelley, led a reflection after each offering. We, who love the taste, shape, and sound of words, sat in the silence between stories. We sat with discomfort and insight and change. And afterward, there was sharing. Tentative, yes, but meaningful.

And, before leaving, all of us, listeners and tellers, signed contracts with ourselves.

We promised concrete, specific changes, in heart, in behavior, in finding and making ways to create a sense of peace.

To have peace, we must nurture the well-being of our entire human family. That nurturing is easy in theory, but difficult to transform into a reality.

Some would find the whole idea of nurturing peace idealistic.

Yes, it is. But how can we possibly strive for anything less?

Now, with this little book packed with stories of wisdom, work and wonder, collected for you to ponder, reflect upon, and share, we begin.

Facing the World, Finding a Way …
A Conversation on Social Media
Lyn Ford

THE FOLLOWING CONVERSATION ON SOCIAL MEDIA prompted Linda Schuyler Ford's "Stories for Peace" programming for the 2016 International Day of Peace. Please note: I haven't used all the messages because some were simply *"yes!"* kinds of statements or agreement with or repetition of what I had asked and said. I've also edited some of the posts for length and changed the order of posts for continuity. Thanks to all who shared your ideas and your hearts:

Lyn Ford's July 7, 2016 post: The news of the past few days angers me, sickens me, and breaks my heart. There is no excuse for blatant inhumanity, and the fear and hatred it propagates. We cannot leave this heritage to our children and grandchildren. **Soooo … with love and respect, not just our dreams but our goals and our responsibility, what do we do?**

Mark Jeffers: What news?

Lynette Ford: Video of the police shooting of Philando Castile last night in Falcon Heights (caught on video by his girlfriend, driver of the car, and witnessed by a child in the back seat) or the shooting of Alton Sterling in a parking lot in Baton Rouge (again, video as evidence). Deaths at the hands of people with power, a certain mindset, and guns. I'm not dissing all officers of the law. I'm speaking to the need for change.

Mark Jeffers: Thank you for the update, I have since looked up these incidents of violence—Jesus the God!

Kiran Flip Singh Sirah: I'd like to have a conversation on this. It's important. Critically. I feel it's important that young people are given the tools to tell their own stories. Lyn. Let's set up a time to talk. In Baton Rouge right now and have met some amazing young people. Gives me hope. Hugs to you.

Carol McCormick: This morning I did two "Art of Storytelling" programs at a suburban daycare center … I shared stories where people were afraid yet chose to act non-violently, and reinforced the message of caring for our *whole* human family as well as animals via songs. I will start writing again for my young (under age 8) children's bully prevention storytelling curriculum. In order to transform society, we need to nurture empathy and compassion at an early age.

Wenny Elrod: I too have a diverse family in several shades of skin color (a reference to those of us who have families from diverse cultures). My concerns for young grandsons reaching their teens and driving age has kept me awake nights. Since 2008, we have been organizing and growing a community organization that provides opportunities for children and families to create (write & tell) stories to improve literacy skills. The participants have been multi-genera-tional and diverse. They have shared their cultures' stories, games, foods, beliefs and more. The children have been guiding lights in moving from fear and violence to acceptance and sharing. Wish this could happen everywhere!!

Donna Marie Kuczynski: We do not learn from our mistakes, we do not profit from history, we repeat and repeat. We do not really try to correct problems of inequality nor face those of poor training of those being trained to protect us … it starts with each of us in our own homes.

Elaine Bleggi: I like what I am reading from all of you. We need to communicate—especially through stories. But we also need to remember two things: first, peace comes from within ourselves and second, we need to pass it on. In other words—teach the children. We are all children of the earth, aren't we?

Adele Browne: I know this is "preaching to the choir," but we really have to keep our minds and hearts open to LOVE one another. We cannot force anyone else to do it, but we can make a difference one heart at a time. When we succumb to hate and fear, the bad guys win.

Faye B. Wooden: Today my heart hurts for the United States of America. Seems to me the thing to do is try to understand from where this devil raises its ugly head and then figure out how to force it back even deeper into the crevice from which it rises....

Virginia Keeping: Gandhi: "Be the change we wish to see in the world."

Oba William King: We Are All One People! Now, More than Ever—We Need Love

Cathy Jo Smith: We speak out. We try to get our Congress-critters to look into what is happening and put people ahead of politics. And we spread the love as best we can.

Anthony Vinson: Vote responsibly? Be more active in our communities? Serve on local boards, committees, and counsels? Volunteer? Be the change we want to see? There's so much that we could do, and so much that we already do.... The trick is how do we grow our tribes, create momentum, and sustain our movements in the midst of living our already packed and sometimes overwhelming lives?! Maybe it's a matter of doing one thing. Just one. And doing it consistently. We all have room for one more thing, right? Sure we do. Bear in mind Plato's (or Mark Twain or Ben Franklin) reminder to, be kind, for everyone is fighting a tough battle. Start there; it's as good a place as any.

Laura Edmonds: Get Louder.

Kristin Pedemonti: My first instinct: be as loving, compassionate and kind as possible in every encounter. Also, post stories about kind interactions to counter the hatred and fear. And vote. And get involved in whatever way possible. We really need to change these very broken systems. Hugs from my heart to yours.

Maria Storyteller: So true, dear Lynette, so true it is a dark cloud all over the world…. BUT WITH LOVE we can change all these.

Lynette Ford: I'm prepping for a library job. My presence, with my dear husband/roadie, and my storytelling in the library will hugely increase the diversity of this community—for an hour. But the stories may plant a little seed of wisdom and understanding in the minds of those who attend. It's the watering, weeding, and nurturing that make a difference.

Lynda Tourloukis: We do more of what we do well. We add another program, reach another individual, we go out and take one step toward the light about what is good and right…. I scheduled more offerings, made more connections and got in touch with a few more people…. when we all do this instead of [wringing] our hands, we accomplish much.

Oba William King: Yes, and I agree. I am grappling with the "Can I do More" … Should I paint a sign and block the road or shout from the city hall steps or continue to send financial support and hope it finds its way … I am committed to telling the stories that heal …

Rory Rennick: I posted this on my wall: HERE WE GO AGAIN! If you FEAR 'BLACK' or FEAR 'BLUE', you'll probably see RED!! FEAR displaces our ability to reason clearly in the moment. No more bloodshed!! Truth can liberate you from most fear.

Sylvia Yancy Davis: Continue to spread the word, educate, love, and pray.

Bynn Sharper: I will speak through my music to my local community. I will be an advocate for diversity and inclusion. I will strive to be the change I want to see in the world.

Kim Cooper Brooks: I am leading prayer meeting tonight at Chapel with that topic in mind. "Peeling the Onions of Community" each layer of hatred, misunderstanding, evil...

Sharon Holley: My question is like yours … I'm praying for answers.

Michelle Frenzer Cornell: Lyn—I hear your outrage and worry. I heard a man on a radio talk show describe his rage as this injustice goes on without end. I felt the power in his indignation. A power that will not take "No" for an answer.

Bobbie Kinkead: OH —> [FYI: the response to this is IO! It's the "Ohio Buckeye" shout out] if you travel to the mid-west—the attitudes are out there. Speak up against them again and again—Do not give in. Stick-up for what is good and helpful.

Sherril Ellis Miller: We counter negativity by spreading love through stories and focusing on your sameness, not division.

Liz Warren: We foster the power of imagination through the stories we tell. Imagination is the key to empathy and compassion. We must be able to imagine ourselves in the positions of others, and then to commit to alleviating the conditions that have brought about the inequities and suffering.

Ted Parkhurst: How can we still the anger and the fear? Stories can help.

"Looking behind, I am filled with gratitude, looking forward,
I am filled with vision, looking upwards I am filled with
strength, looking within, I discover peace."

—Quero Apache Prayer

∞

This Facebook conversation went on for days. Those who responded were storytellers and story lovers, musicians and magicians, poets, preachers, authors in various genres, and friends. I am grateful for their offerings. These were the sparks that lit the fire that burned into a passion to put together this book.

It's a deliberately *little* book but filled with information, examples, and resources for those who speak peace. It's my way of leaving a few little things for my children and grandchildren and great-grandchildren, and all the children of the world—if I can help to plant seeds of promise, perhaps their generations will help to fulfill it.

Part One
Wisdom

WISDOM

"The ability to make reliably sound decisions and come
to well-informed conclusions based on one's processing
of experience, knowledge, and honorable judgment. The
aptitude for discernment of inner qualities and potentially
optimal relationships; insight."

—Lyn Ford

WHEN WE CAN SEE AND FEEL THE CONNECTIONS between the face
in the mirror and the faces of others, we become one with the world
family. But to develop the senses that find and recognize this family,
we must redevelop the open hearts that echo the rhythms of our
childhood trust. We must seek anew that innocence which encouraged us to find playmates with no boundaries set upon who might
play life's games and rituals. We have to develop the combination of
ego-less empathy and common sense that defines both inner peace
and wisdom. And we must assemble the knowledge our task requires.

The wisdom we speak of in our first chapter can also be termed
insight. We acknowledge insight into the actions and words of several
gifted members of the world family. Their experiences have brought
them a clear awareness of the loving ties that should connect all of
us. Perhaps you will find here a spark to light a candle or start a fire
within your own heart and community.

A Conversation

"Cab driver bringing me home from the airport asked, 'Left
or right?'
I said, 'Toward the light' and nodded toward the intersection,
where the light was just turning green.
He repeated, 'Left or right?'
Again I said, 'Toward the light.'
He said, 'No, no, no, Clinton or Trump?'
After a long pause, I gave my response, 'Toward the light.'
He said, 'Ah, yes, now I understand.'
He smiled and nodding knowingly, said, 'You are very wise.'
I was still trying to figure out what I'd said in the first place
that prompted the conversation."
—Lyn Ford, September 23, 2016.

Chapter One

The Promised Land
Linda Schuyler Ford

"By three methods we may learn wisdom: First, by reflection,
which is noblest; Second, by imitation, which is easiest; and
Third by experience, which is the bitterest."
—Confucius

I ARRIVED AT THE VENUE FIVE MINUTES BEFORE SHOW TIME, soaked
from the short walk across the parking lot in a downpour, shell-
shocked by a five-hour drive through the rain on unfamiliar roads,
and feeling utterly unpeaceful.

For a *peace* concert.

I knew there would be four storytellers. A Holocaust survivor
would tell a heart-stopping story of escape, safely told within the
comforting surroundings of the library, in a mansion-like setting
that would accommodate the event. In the sunroom, a woman would
tell about the murder of her son, and her journey to forgiveness. The
hostess, a Muslim woman, planned to divulge the dark realities of
hatred and threats that she met head-on as a new American. I would
be the fourth storyteller.

Four tellers. Twenty minutes each, with four groups of listeners moving from one room to the next every twenty minutes. A round robin. But with gravitas.

And me.

The hostess positioned me in front of a two-story white fireplace. Directly across the room stood a life-sized horse statue, glinting with tiny silver, gold, and white mosaic tiles. Here, I was to tell folktales. *Folk*tales. I felt overwhelmed by my commute, this mansion, the other powerful stories.

But it was time to begin. Now. I smiled as a dozen well-dressed, eager listeners took their seats.

Breathe.

I had planned this carefully, hadn't I? Didn't I know the value, the power of a well-chosen folktale? I had chosen three. Three stories: one about listening, one about changing perspectives, and one about taking action.

We were in the first story. My awful commute was forgotten. All that existed was the story. I saw it reflected in the listeners' eyes. I paced the first tale with the rhythm of their breathing. The white room now glowed softly. Its huge proportions softened, held us gently. Together. In story.

The story I planned to close out each set with was Tim Tingle's *Crossing Bok Chitto*.[1] A story of tremendous strength and grace, it came to me as a gift of grace. First, with Tim's generous permission to tell it, and then with his offer to coach me on the Choctaw version of the spiritual "We Are Bound for the Promised Land"[2] sung in the middle of the story. Tim's generosity and his story are sweet gifts.

I was in my last round of storytelling. The stories that needed to be told were told. Tonight's offerings were pieces of a completed jigsaw puzzle. Each story fulfilled a purpose, contributed to a message. I stepped into the circle of light that is *Crossing Bok Chitto* and felt the story come to life in that room one last time.

The audience was one spirit now. Their empathetic connection was a palpable and profound part of the moment.

I sang the words that Tim had so carefully taught me.

"Umala holitopama
Chiot aya lashke!"

We are bound for the promised land.

A song that, historically, would be sung by Choctaw, slaves and plantation owners. A song that, at that moment, reached straight into the hearts and hopes of everyone in that audience.

And then I saw them, three men, all nodding, standing near each other at the back of the room. Each man wore clothing distinctive to a faith tradition. Muslim. Jewish. Christian. Yet they stood, side by side, all nodding, all embracing the promise of one ultimate home for each of them and all of us.

In that moment, hatred was a wisp of air, easily brushed away with the breath of a story and song. Love was an easy journey, taken on different paths, but with only one destination, one goal, one promise.

Peace.

Notes

1.   *Crossing Bok Chitto: A Choctaw Tale of Friendship & Freedom,* written and told by Tim Tingle. 2008, Cinco Puntos Press, reprint edition.

2.   "We are bound for the promised land" refers to the hymn "On Jordan's Stormy Banks I Stand," by Samuel Stennett (1727-1795), an English Baptist minister. The hymn first appeared as "The Promised Land" in the U.S. in the American collection of William Walker's *The Southern Harmony* (1835) with Stennett's words set to a tune originally in a minor key, by one "Miss M. Durham," about whom we could find no other reference.

The Southern musician, Rigdon M. McIntosh, changed the tune to its major mode, and added its popular refrain directly taken from Stennett's writing:

"I am bound for the promised land. I am bound for the
promised land;
Oh who will come and go with me?
I am bound for the promised land."

This version was published in 1895, in *Gospel Light* by H. R. Christie. It has become the one included in most hymnals since that time.

Chapter Two

Drawing on the Power of Cultural Stories, Human Rights Storytelling, & Dialogue for Peace

Jessica Senehi

"Let no man pull you so low as to hate him."
—Martin Luther King Jr., *A Knock at Midnight: Inspiration from the Great Sermons of Reverend Martin Luther King, Jr.*

You can't hate someone once you know their story (Wheatley). This oft-quoted phrase, perhaps, gets at the heart of the relationship between storytelling and peace, and the rest may be merely commentary.

For a person or group, to not have their story acknowledged is to be invisible and dismissed. Some stories may be more important to acknowledge than others. Unacknowledged loss, argue Kenneth Hardy and Tracey Laszloffy, is the "dehumanization of loss," and contributes to rage.

For the past twenty-five years, I have learned about storytelling from storytellers and those who use story-based approaches for peace-building. From 1993 through 2000, I interviewed more than forty storytellers, many of whom were from the St. Louis area or were featured in the St. Louis Storytelling Festival. Most of these tellers would identify as being part of the storytelling renaissance emerging in North America and Europe in the 1970s (Sobol).

In 2006, in Winnipeg, Manitoba, the Mauro Centre for Peace and Justice at the University of Manitoba, where I have worked since 2003, established the Winnipeg International Storytelling Festival: *Festival du conte de Winnipeg,* based on the St. Louis model. My ideas about storytelling for peace have been further shaped and influenced within a vibrant storytelling and peacemaking community in Winnipeg.

This article offers a definition of peace and some ideas about storytelling for peace. Three different types of storytelling are discussed in terms of their potential for peace: cultural storytelling, human rights storytelling, and dialogue. Considerations for moving forward are shared.

Peace

Peace and conflict studies is a growing interdisciplinary field of teaching, research, and practice. Peace is not merely the absence of war and violence; it is also the presence of social justice. Peace can be considered at multiple levels of analysis: the inner self and the interpersonal, intergroup, and international levels.

This is not to argue that storytelling is inherently good. Storytelling is destructive when dominant discourses do not include groups of people; when stories generate and spread discrimination and hatred; and when stories are part of a process of misrepresentation and denial. Constructive storytelling is inclusive and fosters collaborative power and mutual recognition; creates opportunities for openness, dialogue, and insight; and brings issues to consciousness; or is a means of resistance (Senehi, "Constructive Storytelling: A Peace Process").

Cultural storytelling

Joe McLellan sits in front of a group of second-graders in an area called "Reading in the Round" at the Millennium Library in Winnipeg. He is Métis, tall, about sixty years old. He holds a large drum with an image of a turtle and strikes a steady beat with a stick. He stops abruptly, as if a thought just struck him.

He asks the students, "What does the drum sound like?" He adds that when he asks that question to adults and even Ph.D. students, they typically don't know the answer. In this way, McLellan upends hierarchies and elevates the young people. He demonstrates in a playful way that he can speak truth to power. The children are delighted.

Someone says, "It sounds like a heartbeat!"

While starting to beat the drum softly, McLellan affirms, "Yes," and adds, "See? Children always know the answer." For a while now, he has had the children's attention, and now they are completely with him.

He continues: "The first sound a child hears is the heartbeat of its mother. The heartbeat says, 'I love you.' Every child knows that the heartbeat is saying that their mother loves them."

This story speaks to the universal aspects of humanity. We are all born. Everyone deserves to be loved. Unconditionally. Not because of how they look, how they do in school, or how much money they have, but because of their humanity, the dignity of the human person.

This is the lead-in to Joe McLellan's telling one of his Nanobosho stories. Joe McLellan created a series of Nanobosho books for children so that indigenous young people could see people like themselves in books (McLellan). I'm using the term "cultural storytelling" to refer to the telling of traditional folktales in schools and other public contexts whether or not the teller is from that culture. This has been the main type of story told during the storytelling renaissance during its heyday (roughly 1970 to 2000), though perhaps less so in recent years as more people tell personal stories. This type of story-telling serves as peace-building in several ways: through its content, through the acknowledgment of subordinated groups, through inclusive processes that nurture youth voice, and through nurturing imagination and creating bonds of attachment that foster resilience.

Hearing wisdom stories from one's culture in a mainstream setting is validating and builds self-esteem for those in non-mainstream cultures (e.g., Eisele). Hearing wisdom stories from other cultural groups builds respect across cultures (e.g., Dyson and Geneshi). Such wisdom stories share many insights about inter-personal conflict resolution, ethics, and social justice that can be a resource for young people to think through problems. By identifying with the speaker of the story in a non-confrontational context, young story listeners build their capacity for empathy, which is important for peacemaking (e.g., Fairbairn, Paley).

An inclusive process of storytelling, often practiced by renaissance storytellers, inviting young people to participate in the storytelling and become storytellers themselves nurtures young people's voice (Rubright, Zipes). This is critical for protection from abuse, global citizenship, and creating a culture of human rights. Paying attention to the stories of toddlers helps build family ties, and strengthens the child's language acquisition (Logue, Shelton, Cronkite, and Austin). Telling stories to children can increase a child's vocabulary and bridge the 30-million-word gap, which is the difference in the number of words some children have heard by age three, often as a result of social inequalities (e.g., Trostle and Hicks). Time spent telling stories to children has a nurturing quality, which late storyteller Ruth Windham described as "love" (Senehi). Stories connect the generations; elders tell children stories in a circle that mimics the circle of life.

Human rights storytelling

More than 100 middle-school students entered a room in the Legislature Building during the 2007 Winnipeg International

Storytelling Festival. They were loud, joking with each other, pushing each other, and practically out of control. The teacher asked them to get ready for the storytelling. They continued laughing and talking to each other.

A thin eighty-year-old man, little over five feet tall, rose at the front of the group to speak. He didn't know the students, and they didn't know him. There was no introduction. He just started speaking.

Within moments, except for the voice of the speaker, there was the deep quiet that comes during intense listening. The students were riveted. While the school bus waited outside, the group stayed longer than planned to ask questions and talk with Holocaust survivor and educator, the late Dr. Philip Weiss (1922-2008). The teacher said she was going to invite him to speak to the whole school.

Since it began in 2006, the Winnipeg International Story-telling Festival has featured "human rights storytelling" by people who have experienced the impact of war or human rights violations as children. Human rights and social justice are no longer abstract ideas but flesh-and-blood realities before people's eyes. The telling of such a story can be a transcendent moment of justice when all sense the emergence of a communal spirit that affirms and validates the person who was affected by the loss of their human rights.

Such storytelling is not didactic, but a relating of experiences, implying a more egalitarian relationship between the teller and listeners, which is empowering to young listeners. People affected by trauma risk re-traumatizing with re-telling. Narrative therapists at the Dulwich Centre in Australia have focused on how to "tell stories in ways that make us stronger," which recognize how the special strengths and knowledge that people have demonstrated in responding to difficult times. Human rights storytelling offers a chance to find ways to draw on these processes and model witnessing.

Dialogue

It is a late July afternoon in 2005, and we have been at Tantur, an ecumenical center south of Jerusalem for an all-day training for facilitators involved in a new peace-building project called Jerusalem Stories: Performance, Exhibit, Dialogue.

Twenty facilitators, men and women, of different ages—half of whom are Palestinian and half of whom are Israeli—talk. They have been working for peace for most of their lives. Throughout the day, they share personal history and insights, joke, argue, discuss, and, for the past half hour or so, it seems they mostly despair.

One wall of the room is glass, leading to a terrace overlooking a descending hillside dotted with olive trees. On the hills arising across this valley is the town of Bethlehem, illuminated by the gold hues of the afternoon sun. A blue-green dome sparkles like a jewel among the buildings. Minarets reach skyward. The recently built gray separation wall rings the bottom of the town like an incision.

The facilitators are here to discuss a new initiative developed by storyteller Carol Grosman, seeking to bring the stories of real people into a public context. The project will involve the production of the eight three-hour events, free to the public, each to include (1) a play featuring the real stories of three Palestinians and three Israelis from Jerusalem, (2) an exhibit of twenty-three large portrait photographs of Palestinians and Israelis by photojournalist Lloyd Wolf, and (3) small-group discussions among audience members to be held directly after the performance. There will be two productions of the same play—one in Arabic to be held for Palestinian audiences in East Jerusalem, and one in Hebrew to be held for Israeli audiences in West Jerusalem.

In the room at Tantur, a muezzin's call can be heard from the minaret that rises above Bethlehem's rooftops, followed almost immediately by the singing of a German youth choir in another room of the building, the two sacred melodies beautifully momentarily coexist.

∞

Dialogue processes seek to develop understanding across divides in longstanding, intractable conflicts involve personal storytelling. Sustained dialogue, largely developed by diplomat Harold Saunders, has been used in many contexts and types of settings (also, Parker, Zartman). The process of personal storytelling, which is non-didactic and builds empathy between the listener and teller, is seen to be at the heart of successful process of To Trust and Reflect (Bar-On) addressing the Palestinian-Israeli conflict, Healing through Remembrance in Northern Ireland (O'Hagan), and other bi-communal projects in Northern Ireland (Maiangwa and Byrne 2015). While this may seem like a different process than sharing traditional folktales by people who have worked to develop their storytelling and artistic skills, there may be value in seeing how these forms may interrelate. Dialogue, however, is typically distinguished by a private setting that is confidential for the participants.

Increasingly, artists and peacemakers are drawing on the power of storytelling to bridge the gap across chasms of conflicts defined in identity terms through innovative projects in a public sphere. (Senehi 2018). In her project Jerusalem Stories, Carol Grosman combined personal storytelling, which is similar to human rights storytelling, as people spoke about how they were affected by conflict, with theatre, photography, and dialogue (Senehi). In Theatre of Witness, established by Teya Sepinuck, the personal stories of participants are crafted to a theatre piece that they present. This type of work brings personal stories into a "public transcript," to use James Scott's phrase. The techniques of storytelling create an approach that is often attractive and fascinating while at the same time less threatening and didactic than other approaches. This contributes to the possibility for a transformative shift in how people think about the conflict and each other (Senehi, "Constructive Storytelling: A Peace Process").

∞

The storytelling renaissance, as Sobol put it, has nurtured the art of storytelling in contemporary times. In this cultural movement, there was an emphasis on preserving traditional cultural stories, which—along with other intellectual trends of the 1970s—valued

Indigenous knowledge (e.g., Haley), interrogated how power relations were tied up with the production of knowledge (e.g., Foucault), and sought social change and social justice (e.g., Césaire). This also coincided with "a narrative turn" across disciplines. Going forward, as new intellectual trends and societal priorities emerge, storytelling will continue to be central to how people build identities and knowledge, make sense of the past, "tell the story of now" as Marshall Ganz would put it, and envision the future.

It is okay to combine approaches. Traditionally, stories were not simply vessels of meaning deposited in listeners, but were used by storytellers to analyze and comment on what was happening in the present in order to shape the future (Hale, Scheub, Tonkin). There are innumerable ways to draw on the power of cultural storytelling, human rights storytelling, and dialogue. Deaf storytelling may involve telling a cultural story, and also contribute to a culture of human rights. Someone might draw on the power of cultural storying during a dialogue process.

Create spaces for storytelling. Increasingly, in North American, mass media is balkanized or controlled by powerful media corporations. An environment rich with opportunities for accessible storytelling is important for people's and communities' wellbeing. Storytelling has an important role to play in education at all levels, pre-kindergarten through graduate studies. People might be mindful to create spaces for these types of storytelling in their schools, workplaces, and community centers.

Research. Research is needed to learn more about how people use storytelling, how people respond, and innovative models. For example, Magdalena Wieglhofer provides an analysis of Theatre of Witness. Mundy-Taylor, May, and Reynolds demonstrate how young people concentrate longer to hear stories when storytelling sessions are provided over time. This provides evidence for the use of storytelling for enriching and developing the listening and concentration skills necessary for conflict resolution and peacemaking. Marilyn Berg Iarusso describes how space was made for cultural storytelling at the New York Public Library through their Storytelling Program, established by librarian Anna Cogswell Tyler, in 1907 and, in its heyday, reached 147,000 per year until the program was cut in 2008. Storytelling studies will continue to be an important intersection with peace and conflict studies. There are many questions to explore across disciplines. While storytelling is as old as human history, a continuing process of questioning, research, and innovation will always be needed and of interest.

REFERENCES

Bar-On, D., Ed. (2000) *Bridging the Gap: Storytelling as a Way to Work through Political and Collective Hostilities.* Hamburg, Germany: Körber-Stiftung.

Césaire, A. (1972) *Discourse on Colonialism,* translated by Joan Pinkham. New York: Monthly Review Press.

Denborough, D. (2008) *Collective Narrative Practice.* Adelaide, Australia: Dulwich Centre.

Dyson, A. H. & Genishi, C., Eds. (1994) *The Need for Story: Cultural Diversity in Classroom and Community.* Urbana, IL: National Council of Teachers of English.

Eisele, K. (2001) "Documenting the Then and the Now: Tucson Youth Tell Tucson Stories." https://www.researchgate.net/publication/234755897_Documenting_the_Then_and_the_Now_Tucson_Youth_Tell_Tucson_Stories January 2001: 16–20.

Fairbarin, G. (2002) "Ethics, Empathy, and Storytelling in Professional Development." *Learning in Health and Social Care* 1.1: 22-32.

Foucault, M. (1972) *The Archaeology of Knowledge and the Discourse on Language,* translated by A.M. Sheridan Smith. New York: Vintage Books.

Ganz, M. (2010) "Leading Change: Leadership, Organization, and Social Movements." *Handbook of Leadership Theory and Practice,* Nohria and Kurana, Eds. Danvers, MA: Harvard Business Press, 509–550.

Hale, T. (1998) *Griots and Griottes: Masters of Words and Music.*

Bloomington, IN: Indiana University Press.

Haley, A. (1976) *Roots: The Saga of an American Family*. New York: Doubleday.

Hardy, K. & Laszloffy, T. (1995) *Teens Who Hurt: Clinical Interventions to Break the Cycle of Adolescent Violence*. New York: Guilford.

Iarusso, M. B. (2016) "Stories: A List of Stories to Read Aloud—The History of the New York Public Library's Storytelling List." *Storytelling Self Society* 12.1: forthcoming.

Logue, M. E., Shelton, H., Cronkite, D. & Austin, J. (2007) "Family Ties: Strengthening Partnerships through Toddlers' Stories." *Young Children* 62.2: 85–87.

Maiangwa, B. & Byrne, S. (2015) "Peace-building and Reconciliation through Storytelling in Northern Ireland and the Border Counties of the Republic of Ireland." *Storytelling, Self, Society* 11.1: 85–110.

Maoz, I. (2000) "Expectations, Results and Perspectives: The Evaluation Report." *Bridging the Gap*, edited by Daniel Bar-On. Hamburg, Germany: Körberg-Stiftung, 135–164.

McLellan, J. (2010) *Nanabosho and the Butterflies*. Winnipeg, MB, Canada: Pemmican.

McLellan, J. (1995) *Nanobosho and the Woodpeckers*. Winnipeg, MB, Canada: Pemmican.

McLellan, J. (2012) *Niki and Wapus Save the People*. Winnipeg, MB, Canada: Pemmican

Mundy-Taylor, J., May, J. & Reynolds, R. (2015) "Storytelling in 3D: Interrogating Engagement with Oral Storytelling in the School Classroom." *Storytelling, Self, Society* 11.2: 159–182.

O'Hagan, L. (2008) *Stories in Conflict*. Handout at YES! Preconference, 2008.

Paley, V. G. (1999) *The Kindness of Children*. Boston, MA: Harvard University Press.

Parker, P. N. (2006) "Sustained Dialogue: How Students Are Changing Their Own Racial Climate." *About Campus* (March–April): 17–23.

Rubright, L. (1996) *Beyond the Beanstalk: Interdisciplinary Learning through Storytelling.* Portsmouth, NH: Heinemann.

Ryan, P. (1995) *Storytelling in Ireland: A Re-awakening.* Derry, Northern Ireland: The Verbal Arts Centre.

Saunders, H. (1999) *A Public Peace Process: Sustained Dialogue to Transform Social and Ethnic Conflicts.* New York: St. Martin's Press.

Scheub, H. (1998) *Story.* Madison, WI: University of Wisconsin Press.

Senehi, J. (2002) "Constructive Storytelling: A Peace Process." *Peace and Conflict Studies* 9.2: 41–63.

Senehi, J. (2000) "Constructive Storytelling: Building Community, Building Peace." Dissertation, Syracuse University.

Senehi, J. (2017) "Story-Based Inter-Group Mediation." Georgakopoulos, A., Ed. *The Mediation Handbook: Research, Theory and Practice.* London, UK: Routledge, 29–36.

Sepinuk, T. (2014) *Theatre of Witness: Finding the Medicine in Stories of Suffering, Transformation and Peace.* London, UK: Jessica Kingsley.

Sobol, J. D. (1999) *The Storytellers' Journey: An American Revival.* Champaign, IL: University of Illinois Press.

Trostle, S. & Hicks, S.J. (1998) "The Effects of Storytelling versus Story Reading on Comprehension and Vocabulary Knowledge of British Primary School Children." *Reading Improvement* 35.3: 127–136.

Weiglhofer, M. (2015) "Who Am I Without My Story? Uncertainties of Identity (Presentation) in Performed Autobiographical Storytelling." *Storytelling, Self, Society* 11.2: 264–280.

Wheatley, M. (2002) *Turning to One Another: Simple Conversations to Restore Hope to the Future.* Oakland, CA: Berrett-Koehler.

Zartman, J. (2008) "Negotiation, Exclusion and Durable Peace: Dialogue and Peace-building in Tajikistan. *International Negotiation* 13: 35–77.

Zipes, J. (1995) *Creative Storytelling: Building Community, Changing Lives.* London, UK: Routledge.

Chapter Three

Excerpt from "Peace XVIII"
Khalil Gibran

"DO NOT BE FRIGHTENED, FOR I AM NOW TRUTH, spared from swords and fire to reveal to the people the triumph of Love over War. I am Word uttering introduction to the play of happiness and peace."

Then the young man became speechless and his tears spoke the language of the heart; and the angels of Joy hovered about that dwelling, and the two hearts restored the singleness which had been taken from them.

At dawn the two stood in the middle of the field contemplating the beauty of Nature injured by the tempest. After a deep and comforting silence, the soldier said to his sweetheart, "Look at the Darkness, giving birth to the Sun."

Kahlil Gibran (1883–1931) was a poet, writer, and artist of Lebanese heritage, born in Bsharri, Ottoman Empire. When Gibran was a young man, he and his family immigrated to the United States. Still considered a literary hero in Lebanon, Gibran wrote his works in both English and Arabic (Waterfield). Gibran is the third best-selling poet of all time, outsold only by William Shakespeare and Lao-Tzu (Acocella).

References

Waterfield, Robin. *Prophet: The Life and Times of Kahlil Gibran.* St. Martin's Press, 1998.

Acocella, Joan. "Prophet Motive," *The New Yorker,* January 7, 2008. http://www.newyorker.com/magazine/2008/01/07/prophet-motive

Chapter Four

Look Who Came Up the Beanstalk

Doug Lipman

"A healthy social life is found only when in the mirror of each soul the whole community finds its reflection, and when in the whole community the virtue of each one is living."

—Rudolf Steiner

WHEN I SAW HER IN THE SIXTH-GRADE CLASSROOM, I WAS SURPRISED.

It was the first day after spring vacation. After eight weeks "in residence," I thought I knew every child in the school. But there she was, an unfamiliar face in the third row.

I said, "Hi! I'm Doug. I'm the storyteller. What's your name?"

No answer.

The boy in the right front desk said, "She doesn't speak; she's French."

Calling on my two semesters of college French, I said, "Bonjour! Je m'appelle Doug."

Framed in her shoulder-length, dark hair, her face lit up as she returned the greeting in French.

I would have added the French words for "I'm the storyteller," but I didn't know them. True, I'd had two semesters of French—but they were both first-semester French. I could only make a few simple statements in the present tense.

My stomach sank. I had a new student who didn't understand a word of English and six storytelling sessions to go. But I had been hired by this well-to-do suburban school to use storytelling as a tool to teach the subject of diversity. I wasn't going to shirk from the added challenge of telling to a more-diverse class.

That day, I told my story largely to the French student. I exaggerated my tone of voice and used as much body language as I could. I looked at her after each line of the story to see if she understood. When she did, she rewarded me with a golden smile. When she didn't, her face showed her puzzlement—and I tried again with an added pantomime for her and a new set of words for the rest of the class. When all else failed, I tried to use a French word as an additional clue for her.

Telling to the One Who Doesn't Understand

By the third session, I appreciated what an extraordinary listener she was. Her face was a perfect mirror for my story. Now I looked at her as much as possible while I told, not just for her, but for my pleasure in a supremely alert, encouraging listener.

In this session, I got stuck making her understand a crucial part of the story. Mime failed me, as did my minuscule French vocabulary. Then I had an idea. "Would someone look that word up for me in the French dictionary?"

Silence. The teacher's look seemed to tell me of too many demands on her, of helplessness at being saddled with this disadvantaged student so late in the year, and of resentment that I should expect her to have a special dictionary for an inconvenient, late-entering student who didn't even speak English.

The boy in the right front desk said, "We don't have one." I stopped in shock, feeling the enthusiasm drain out of my body.

I had been proud of this school, which had chosen storytelling as its art form for the year and diversity as its theme. But now a breathing piece of diversity had flown across the ocean and landed in this classroom, and the school couldn't be bothered to have a French dictionary!

The next time I showed up to tell stories, the boy in the right front desk held up a French dictionary. "Look," he said. "I got it from the library. But it's hard to find the words fast enough."

I said, "Thank you. You are a good friend."

That day, I had prepared "Jack and the Bean Tree," an Appalachian variant of the familiar English classic "Bean Stalk" folktale.

The telling went well. All the children were with Jack and me as we explored the world in the clouds. At the end, they applauded.

Then the French girl raised her hand.

Five Words That Changed Us All

I was so surprised to see her hand go up that I didn't say a word. She had never initiated communication with me.

I called on her. Slowly, she said five words in French, the longest phrase she had so far tried out on me. I repeated what I heard. She said it again, correcting my mispronunciation.

I hadn't understood any of it the first time. But now I caught the first word, "Jacques," and wrote it on the blackboard. Trying to involve the rest of the class in my decoding process, I said aloud, "Like Freré Jacque."

As I said it, I recognized the last word, too. "Magique?" I asked. She nodded. This sounded like French for "magic." I wrote "Magique" on the board.

What were the words in the middle? I said to her, "Jacques, hmmm-mm, hmmm-mm-mm, magique." She repeated the whole phrase. It sounded to me like "et le" ("and the") followed by an unfamiliar word that started with a "Z" sound. I wrote "et le Z" between the other two words.

She shook her head bemusedly and gestured toward the board. With my nodded permission, she went to the board, erased the "Z" and wrote "s H-a-r-i-c-o-t."

At that moment, I thanked the stars for my interest in the folk music of North America. One kind of music I had been drawn to was the French Louisiana style called Zydeco. I had read that "Zydeco" was a misspelling of the first two words of an early song in that style, "Les Haricots ("The Beans …")

Trying to hold the interest of the rest of the class, I said the entire phrase aloud, "Jacque et les Haricot Magique."

Stories Bring Us Together

Just a moment after understanding what I was reading, I spoke the English equivalent. My voice caught: "Jack and the Magic Beans." I just stood there, facing the board.

There was silence in the room behind me. It was that special silence that only falls when an entire group grasps something, all in the same instant. It took my breath away.

All at once, we understood that "Jack and the Beanstalk" is a story with a secret life in other worlds. We understood that the Appalachian "Bean Tree" shares something with people who didn't seem to have any stories, with people in some place called France, with people who "don't speak".

These people, we realized together, also fear for simple heroes facing terrible giants. They somehow have magic beans in their imaginations, just like we have in ours.

We understood, deep in our bellies, how stories are stitches that hold humanity together.

I don't know if my other lessons that year had any effect. I don't know if the other classes in that school ever made a connection between my folktales and their lives.

But that one day, in that one class, I know that—without any intention on my part—multiculturalism actually climbed the thick-trunked vine of story and emerged, dazed and breathless, into the far-away castle of our classroom.

Chapter Five

Shaping Young Minds for Social Justice within Educational Standards

Celine O'Malley

"WHAT IS IT THAT WE REALLY NEED TO SURVIVE?"

I posed this question to my first graders last month, as we began our unit on economics, part of the California Common Core curriculum for their grade level. I had just gathered them on the carpet around our "campfire" to tell them a story of a little woman who lived in a shoebox (my adaptation of the tale *The Little Old Woman who lived in a Vinegar Bottle*). The little woman is never satisfied with what she has and always wants more, only to realize in the end that what she really needed she had from the very beginning, and what she wanted didn't actually end up being what truly made her happy anyway. The story was our unit's foundation for establishing the difference between a want and a need, one of the basic economic concepts needed to build on for further understanding.

As a student teacher in the bilingual program at Chico State this last year, I spent many hours reading and discussing a multicultural, social justice lens on teaching. When I found out that one of the units I was going to be teaching was on economics, my head was filled with grand visions of lessons on cooperative living, alternative economies, economic inequity and people-powered economic revolutions. Then I remembered, I teach first grade. These were six- and seven-year-olds; would be establishing the basic concepts: a want versus a need, a good versus a service, a producer versus a consumer. But six-year-olds are already learning that you can't always get what you want. My goal with the unit was to instill a deeper understanding of how oftentimes we can't always get what we **need** either, and some more so than others.

At first, I felt concerned—was I going to be radicalizing their young spongy minds with my social justice "radical" leanings? Would their parents come marching over and demand I be removed as the student teacher? And then, I decided that was okay. My job as an educator, as a storyteller, is to expand my students' minds, to teach critical thinking, and expose students to a wide range of ideas and realities, making sure that the perspectives are varied and that the voices and stories that have long been silenced are given time to speak. For these very reasons, stories are the perfect way to enter into social justice explorations.

For students to understand inequity, they first had to understand the difference between a want and a need. This was a rich opportunity to teach **empathy**, and establish an awareness of differences within our classroom community. I would teach that everyone deserves to be treated with **kindness** and have access to basic necessities to survive. After our introductory story, and discussing this with the children, we launched our unit. We learned about situations where people don't have what they need to survive. We wrote letters to children in Syrian refugee camps and heard stories from a Syrian refugee art teacher who came to speak to our class. We learned about trade-offs and making decisions, and how those decisions affect our lives and others' lives as well. At the end of the unit, students still returned to our story of the little woman who lived in the shoebox and the basic needs that we established through that story--shelter, clean water, healthy food, fresh air, and someone who cares.

Whether it is a story to kick-start a unit, a story amidst the day's lessons to reinforce concepts being learned, or having students hear the stories of people who can bring our classroom learning back out to the real world (where students live their everyday lives in their communities), storytelling is a powerful tool in the social justice toolbox for education.

NOTE

This article was first printed in the 2016 journal of the Youth, Education, and Storytellers Alliance of the National Storytelling Network, *Storytelling and Social Justice*, edited by Lyn Ford.

Chapter Six

Beginner's Peace

Bob Kanegis

"Knowledge speaks, but wisdom listens"
—Jimi Hendrix

"The Only Thing We Have to Fear Is Fear Itself"
I can't read or hear this most famous of quotes by President Franklin Roosevelt, uttered at the height of the Second World War, without simultaneously hearing the words of a nine-year-old girl, one of our students in the Visions and Voices Project.

"I *Am* Fear," she said. Though likely this was a grammatical construction of a girl whose English was a second language trying to express that she was afraid to speak in public, the idea that one could actually *be the embodiment of an emotion* led me to ask if it might be possible to *be* peace.

I started thinking consciously about peace back in the mid-1950s in elementary school while we were doing duck-and-cover drills in those early Cold War days. Two things I remember clearly about that time: I experienced frequent nightmares about mushroom clouds, and I was curious about why several of my class-mates did not participate in the drills. Instead, while we assumed the futile protective position in the hallways, these third-grade refuse-niks marched off to the principal's office. Years later they were able to explain to me that their parents felt that to participate was to feed war mentality. The family of one of these classmates, still a good friend after all these years, sponsored the monk and peace advocate Thich Nhat Hanh when he was exiled from Vietnam for his anti-war activities. Among the many books that Thich Nhat Hanh has written is one called *Being Peace*.

It was President Franklin Roosevelt who first coined the term "United Nations," although he did not live to see the institution's creation. He died only a few months before delegates met in San Francisco to work out the text of the U.N. Charter, which was signed on June 26, 1945. On May 5th of that year, at the suggestion of the Redwood League, the conference delegates took a break and visited nearby Muir Woods National Monument to honor Roosevelt. Here, in such a 'temple of peace,' suggested the Redwood League, the delegates would also gain a perspective and sense of time and human history that could be obtained "nowhere in America better than in a forest that was already mature when the Magna Carta was signed."

Fifty years later, in collaboration with the United Nations Association, Muir Woods, and a number of local schools, we celebrated the anniversary of that historic occasion with the Vision and Voices Project. For six weeks, we worked with students creating beautiful-ly-written and illustrated scrolls that expressed the students' dreams and hopes for peace. On the morning of May 5th, students and their families gathered in Cathedral Grove, holding hands in a huge circle, listening silently to the sound of a Tibetan bell, then reverently tying their scrolls to the redwoods. Later that evening U.N. delegates and staff walked to the grove, found the scrolls, read them to each other and then took one home as a gift and talisman from the students.

At that moment, I felt like I was part of something big. A project with the United Nations! I hadn't felt that personal connec-tion to a historic event since I'd traveled to Washington to participate in the anti-war protests of the sixties.

One of the through-lines in my adult life has been a persistent feeling of not doing enough, or that what I have done is not making a big enough impact. In some ways, I suppose that is an occupational hazard of being a storyteller. On one level we sense or know or feel that we are connecting to minds and hearts, but those clear-cut, unambiguous occasions when we know on a deep level don't come as often as our egos clamor for, at least not mine. So, what would it really take for me to be able to say, yes, I am an active and effective advocate and contributor to the Peace Movement?

∞

I was not Peace. I was Fear! Several weeks after the attack on 9/11, I was drinking coffee at one of the sidewalk tables outside The French Hotel, a favorite java joint in Berkeley. I looked up from the book I was reading and was alarmed to see an "Arab-looking" man, fast approaching, obviously distressed, furtively looking first one way and then the other. As hard as I tried to avoid falling prey to stereotypes and jumping to conclusions, I felt a gathering anxiety about his behavior and intentions. I became Fear when I realized he was making a beeline to my table. He was coming for me! Then in a flash, there he was, looking straight in my eyes with his anxious demeanor.

"Excuse me please, sir," he said. "I was sitting at this table a few minutes ago and I seem to have lost my keys. I wonder if I may have left them here?"

Whew! Here was a chance for redemption (in my own eyes) and an opportunity to transform myself from paranoid and suspicious neighborhood watchman to helpful citizen. "Let me help you look," I offered. "Do you think you may have left them here near the cafe?" I rose from my chair, ready to jump into action. Magically the keys appeared—right on the chair where I'd been sitting!

That's when I remembered the story of Nasruddin and his lost keys. Nasruddin, the hero of countless Sufi stories, is sometimes the fool, sometimes the wise one, and sometimes a baffling combination of both.

A Story of Nasruddin

There he was one evening, on his hands and knees, searching for his keys under a lamplight near the village square. Soon a small crowd of Good Samaritans joined in the search... But to no avail. The keys could not be found.

"Mullah, are you quite sure you lost them here?"

"Oh no, no, no, not here, I don't think I lost the keys near here," Nasruddin replied, not looking up, as he continued crawling around on all fours. "I lost the keys when I was working in the garden this afternoon."

"Then why in the world are you looking for them here the street?" asked one of the now incredulous members of the search party.

"Can't you see?" said Nasruddin. "The light is much, much better here!"

And so the "terrorist" walked on, happy to be reunited with his keys, and I was left with a story and a snippet of a song. I asked myself, *have I been looking for peace in all the wrong places,* when that peace was right under my butt, so to speak, right where I was sitting or standing at any given moment? Yes, if I wanted to be part of a peace movement, I'd have to *move,* look closer to home, look, in fact, *right at myself.*

Then I remembered another story. This, by the way, is what I call "story fever": the incurable and chronic condition of constantly connecting stories to life and life to stories. The story was one attributed to a giant in the peace movement, Mahatma Gandhi.

A Mother Brought Her Young Son to Gandhi

It is said that a mother brought her young son to Gandhi, and complained that he ate too much sugar. "Tell him," she pleaded, "to stop eating sugar. Tell him that it's not good for him."

"I cannot do that," Gandhi replied, "but please return with the child in two weeks."

Two weeks later, the mother and child returned. Again, the mother pleaded for Gandhi's support.

"Stop eating sugar child," Gandhi said. "Your mother is right. It is not good for you."

The woman was thankful but perplexed. "Sir … why couldn't you have told my son to stop eating sugar when I first asked for your help?"

"Because, Madam," said Gandhi, "two weeks ago, I was still eating sugar."

With visions of Nasruddin and Gandhi swirling in my mind, I determined to be a man of peace, starting first with myself, then with my family, then community, in ever-widening circles. But, first, peace with myself. Yes. First, I would learn to Be Peace.

Since that day, now many years ago, I can confidently say that I have lost the peace each and every day. I have lost the peace countless thousands of times! "Peace, how do I lose you, let me count the ways!"

I lose the peace arguing with the phone company. I lose it when the clerk in the store seems disengaged. I lose the peace when I am thwarted, insulted, ignored, when things don't go as expected, when I don't get my way. I lose the peace when I growl back in anger at the neighbors' dogs' incessant barking. I lose it when I want to flip the bird to that jerk tailgating me on the freeway. I lose it yelling at the television over the latest outrage by the latest jerk of a politician. I lose the peace when I take it "poisonally" if someone questions my judgment, or offers a critique of a hard-held position of mine. I lose the peace by making assumptions about people, stereotyping them, reacting to them when I don't like the look on their face or the look they gave me.

But I think most telling and most damaging to me and others is that, once having lost it, I find it difficult to regain the peace, and to get back to a feeling of equanimity. It's not that I want to hold on to grudges. More often I'm not even aware that that is just what I'm doing … that long after the storm of a moment's conflict has passed, I'm still holding on to an unpleasant feeling. How does that serve me? How does that serve the peace? In those moments, I am anger, I am intolerance, I am frustration, irritation, and anxiety. And sometimes, yes, *I am* Fear.

If there is any good news in this litany of losing the peace, it is that having lost it, one always has the opportunity to find it again. In the parlance of Zen Buddhism, one tries to keep "beginners mind." "In the beginner's mind there are many possibilities, in the expert's mind, there are few" (from the introduction to *Zen Mind, Beginner's Mind* by Shunryu Suzuki).

I have a treasured first edition boxed copy of another Zen classic, *Zen Flesh, Zen Bones* by Paul Reps, that includes 101 Zen stories. Several of the stories have become almost like talismans and touchstones for me in my attempts to walk in my own personal peace march. There's a Zen tradition of the master giving a student a whack on the head if he senses the student lost in thought or dozing. The stories have a similar effect on me, bringing me back to the present, back to myself when I am in danger of losing myself in a moment of conflict, confusion, or inattention, in those moments when I suddenly realize I've been holding a stale grudge. Here are two of those stories … stories that come unbidden to mind in times when I have lost the peace.

The Muddy Road

Two monks were once traveling together down a muddy road. A heavy rain was falling. Coming around a bend, they met a lovely young girl wearing a silk kimono, unable to cross a flooded intersection.

Come, girl." said Tanzan without hesitation. He picked her up and carried her over the swollen waters.

The other monk did not speak again until later that night when they reached their temple. Then he no longer could restrain himself. "We monks don't go near females," he scolded his companion, "especially not young and beautiful ones. Did you forget our precepts?"

"I left the girl back there at the intersection," said Tanzan. "Are you still carrying her?"

Liz, my storytelling partner and wife, and I once found ourselves in the middle of a heated exchange about the appropriateness of a story for a group of teen moms we were working with. When Liz offered her take, it made absolutely no sense to me and I countered with what I was sure was an unassailable argument. I sensed victory! Liz didn't miss a beat.

"You're right!" she said. "I disagree with my previous statement!" At that moment, with the story of the Muddy Road as a compass, was born what we now call the "Practice of Never-Mind"— the ability to change your mind without feeling threatened, to let go of hardened positions and the heat that is generated in defending them. When we can stop carrying an idea, or a strongly-held position, when we can recognize in a flash that we are holding a grudge or stale emotion, we join the Peace March. The key is to strengthen one's skill at actually becoming aware of what you are holding onto.

The Difference Between Heaven and Hell

A soldier came to the Zen master, Hakuin.

"I want to know about heaven and hell. Do they really exist? What is the difference between them?"

Hakuin looked at the soldier and asked, "Who are you?"

"I am a samurai," announced the proud warrior.

"Ha!" exclaimed Hakuin. "You a soldier? You look more like a beggar and a brute. What makes you think you can understand such insightful things as Heaven and Hell? Go away and do not waste my time with your foolish questions," Hakuin waved his hand dismissively.

The enraged samurai couldn't take Hakuin's insults. He drew his sword.

"Oh, look at that," said Hakuin countered, without losing his composure for a moment, "You have a sword!" Then he continued, "Here now open the gates of Hell."

The samurai was taken aback. Humbled by the discipline and wisdom of Hakuin, he put away his sword and bowed before the Zen Master.

"And here now open the gates of Heaven," said Hakuin.

Wag More, Bark Less... That's what the bumper sticker proclaims on my car. One day as I was pulling out of a very quiet cross street into traffic, I was violently jolted by a car that rear-ended me. The other driver and I jumped out of our vehicles at the same time. The woman immediately asked if I was okay, then quickly began to apologize.

"It's all my fault," she said. "I loved the message on your bumper sticker so much that I was trying to write it down when I hit you."

You blooming idiot, I thought! Writing, driving, and not paying attention! The gates of hell opened.

Then I remembered the bumper sticker. "Bark Less," it said, and here I was barking mad. I sheathed the sword.

"Lady, I want to scream at you! But the bumper sticker won't let me!" At that moment, we had a good laugh together. We marched together in the Peace Movement.

As I write this today, tensions are rising again on the Korean Peninsula. The leaders of the United States and North Korea posture, issue threats, and ultimatums, and even declare their willingness to use nuclear weapons. Mutually assured destruction is still a tool of so-called diplomacy. Nuclear nightmares return.

I never found out which of the U.N diplomats took home the one Visions and Voice peace scroll that I remember most vividly. Two boys stand side by side with a dark menacing cannon between them pointed at the boy on the left. The one on the right has his hand near the trigger. But the boy on the left has a smile on his face. "Stop the War!" he says. The boy on the right, too young to read Zen parables, nevertheless knows how to sheath his sword. "Okay!" he replies. This was the earnest and innocent expression of an 8-year-old, already on the peace path. A child *being peace.*

There are a hundred ways to lose the peace and start a war and a hundred ways to find the peace and stop the war every day. When we lose the peace and draw the sword, we can put it back. When we demand peace from others, we can ask ourselves if we have stopped eating sugar. If we look to others to make the peace, we can wink at Nasruddin's folly. We can ask ourselves what we carry that holds us back. We can return to Beginner's Mind. To be in the peace movement, we have to move towards peace. No act, no thought, no movement is too small. Stop the War. Be Peace.

Notes & Resources

Hanh, T. N. (2009) *Being Peace*. Berkley, CA: Parallax Press.

Reps, P. & Senzaki, N. (1998) *Zen Flesh, Zen Bones: A Collection of Zen and Pre-Zen Writings*. North Clarendon, VT: Tuttle.

Suzuki, S. & Dixon, T. (1973) *Zen Mind, Beginner's Mind: Informal Talks on Zen Meditation and Practice*. Boulder, CO: Shambala.

"The Difference Between Heaven and Hell" is a Zen koan—a story of an exchange between a Zen master and his disciple. Gyomay M. Kubose's *Zen Koans* (Contemporary Books, 1973) includes a faithful translation of this parable.

"The Muddy Road" is a Zen koan, found in many sources, including Paul Reps' *Zen Flesh, Zen Bones* (Tuttle, 1998).

"A Mother Brought Her Young Son to Gandhi" is perhaps apocryphal but widely told. It is recounted in Gary Burnson's *Lead* (Korn/Ferry International, 2013).

"A Story of Nasruddin" is a Sufi tale from the Middle East. Heather Forest retells it in *Wisdom Tales from Around the World* (August House, 1996) as "Looking for the Key."

All stories included in this article are adaptations by Bob Kanegis.

Chapter Seven

The Cold Within
Bobby Norfolk

As it is with all storytellers, I am always in search of the right story for the right moment. Sometimes, that story falls right into your lap!

Several years ago, as I prepared my keynote for the Sharing the Fire Conference, sponsored by New England Storytelling (NEST), I was in that position: searching for the perfect concluding piece.

Two weeks before the conference, I arrived at a high school for a couple of performances. Student aides escorted me to the arts complex where the performances would be held, and a helpful stage technician walked me through the backstage area before our sound and light check.

As I waited for the students to assemble, I returned to the dressing room for a quiet moment before the show and noticed a blank sheet of green paper on a small table, spotlighted by a track light from above. The illumination allowed me to see that something was written on the reverse side, so I turned it over. Once I did so, my quest ended: there was a powerful poem, attributed to "Anonymous."

Many poets are called "Anonymous," when, perhaps, with a little extra work, their names can be rediscovered and honored. My research later uncovered the real poet, James Patrick Kinney.

The poem was written in the 1960s and rejected by many publishers before it first appeared in *Liguorian,* a Catholic magazine. It is in the public domain.

This is the poem that closed my keynote at the NEST conference, and which has become a staple in my repertoire. Its potent message, delivered through simple words and evocative images, is a stark reminder of the urgent need for love and compassion in our world.

THE COLD WITHIN
by James Patrick Kinney

Six humans trapped by happenstance
In dark and bitter cold
Each one possessed a stick of wood,
Or so the story's told.

Their dying fire in need of logs,
The first woman held hers back.
For on the faces around the fire,
She noticed one was black.

The next man looking cross the way,
Saw one not of his church,
And couldn't bring himself to give
The fire his stick of birch.

The third one sat in tattered clothes,
He gave his coat a hitch.
Why should his log be put to use,
To warm the idle rich?

The rich man just sat back and thought
Of the wealth he had in store.
And how to keep what he had earned
From the lazy, shiftless poor.

The black man's face bespoke revenge
As the fire passed from sight,
For all he saw in his stick of wood

Was a chance to spite the white.

The last man of this forlorn group
Did naught except for gain
Giving only to those who gave
Was how he played the game.

The logs held tight in death's still hands
Was proof of human sin.
They didn't die from the cold without,
They died from—THE COLD WITHIN.

Chapter Eight

"You jeopardize your own tomorrow..."

Excerpted from "The Dangerous Rise of Populism: Global Attacks on Human Rights Values"

Kenneth Roth

IT IS PERHAPS HUMAN NATURE THAT IT IS HARDER TO IDENTIFY with people who differ from oneself, and easier to accept [the] violation of their rights ... But rights by their nature do not admit an à la carte approach. You may not like your neighbors, but if you sacrifice their rights today, you jeopardize your own tomorrow, because ultimately rights are grounded on the reciprocal duty to treat others as you would want to be treated yourself.

Chapter Nine

Ripples and Intersections: Two Meditations on Poetry and Peace

Caryn Mirriam-Goldberg

How Poetry Ripples Across Our Lives

A PEBBLE TOSSED INTO THE WATER SENDS RIPPLES that can overtake the pond for a moment or longer, showing us something new and in motion, ancient and coming to stillness. The same is true with us, especially when that pebble is a poem. Poetry, like storytelling and other Transformative Language Arts (the spoken and written word for social and personal transformation), can ripple across people, places, ideologies, ethnicities, traditions, mindsets, and other wide gulfs to show us our innate interconnectedness. After all, according to scientists, humans share over 99% of the same genome, including our many differences which sometimes strike out in sharp and even violent contrast.

We can better bridge those differences when we see across the gulfs between us how much we often dwell in matching grief, joy, anger, calm, and especially the possibility of a better world, which Emily Dickinson beckons her words, "I dwell in Possibility—/A fairer House than Prose." Poetry can be such a bridge to new possibilities for seeing and being. I remember how Sharon, a student of mine, whose mother had just died, found great comfort in the line "What falls away is always. And is near" from Theodore Roethke's poem, "The Waking." Sharon told me how that short line encapsulated how her grief and love—the sense of her mother's presence and absence—were always near, something I've since understood more deeply with the death of my father and other loved ones. This snippet of poetry names for me the most succinct truth I can fathom about our dead beloveds. Poetry has a knack for telling us about the essential human story in such concise ways that it's no wonder we carry bits of lines and poems in our hearts, and in Sharon's case, engraved on a pendant she always wears.

Through the mirror of the poem, we can see our own stories and moments reflected back to us in stunning clarity. Such clarity and deep seeing make sense since poetry, like storytelling, is rooted in our oral tradition, which echoes back to how the poetic power of words strung together so that we never forget them can help us pass on messages about who we are and how we are to live. If this sounds a lot like what myth does, it's because it is: myth and poetry come out of the same soulful impulse to use language as a kind of blueprint to bring us back to what's universal and, at times, even beyond the changing whims and dictates of culture. The oral tradition is *mythopoetic*, using poetic devices to pass on some essence of what it means to be human.

Those poetic devices include rhythm, rhyme, alliteration, assonance, and other ways words stick together to make them easy to remember and pass on. It's no surprise that our oldest remnants of the oral tradition are found in poems, songs, stories, and chants that can be easily absorbed, memorized, and recited, such as the old English tale of Beowulf that uses driving rhythms and repetition of sounds, or an Aborigine's song lines that link strands of singing to specific paths across the land to name the specific and mythic dimensions of the route. Poetic language makes its own music, enabling humans to pass it on without writing it down. We can even see this in our earliest songs, poems, and stories embedded in our memories, from

"Tora Lora Lora" to Mother Goose rhymes to "The Three Little Pigs" to name some of what carries through from my childhood.

A lot of poetry today, in a world where the written word has often outpaced the spoken one, doesn't need to be packed tight in rhyme or song, yet is still a musical and visual art. Likewise, poetry and stories have always been made of images from the get-go. The specificity of an image speaks to our senses and invites us into the poem. Aristotle explains in his theory of poetry that "The aim of poetry is to represent the universal through the particular, to give a concrete and living embodiment of universal truth." William Carlos Williams tells us the poet's business is "...not to talk in vague categories but to write particularly, as a physician works upon a patient, upon the thing before him in the particular to discover the universal."

Ironically enough, we can only scale the universal through the specific. The precise image shows us a larger world because the image is one unique moment caught in time. I compare this to how, when you enter a house for the first time, you wouldn't necessarily spark a lot of memories, insights, yearnings, and discoveries if the house has no walls, furniture, or knick-knacks picked up from a vendor on a humid day in Paraguay. Imagine, in the living room, someone placing a bluish pink stone, perfectly oval and smooth to the touch, in your palm, and telling you this stone is from a sub-zero day walking along the shore of Lake Superior one February when she was heart-broken over the loss of a dear friend, and your heart and mind might just open in new ways, invoking your own experiences with beauty, loss, nature, rocks, and water. This is how a poem works.

The specificity of a poem is a direct protest about the vague and general rhetoric of war and other forms of violence. As Natalie Goldberg writes in *Writing Down the Bones: Freeing the Writer Within*, "Recording the details of our lives is a stance against bombs with their mass ability to kill, against too much speed and efficiency... Our task is to say a holy yes to the real things of our life as they exist...." She goes on to say that accepting things as they are, and coming "to love the details" is a yes to the reality of the world that helps us overcome some of the noes that suppress the details of our lives. In other words, poems, through precise details, put our particular truth out there in our collective discourse—the chirping bluejay on a high swaying branch on a 100-degree morning in Kansas while Congress threatens to repeal Obamacare and the year's temperature breaks new records—so that the real light and shadows, heartbreaks, and breakthroughs of our lives have their voice alongside whatever the news is replaying every thirty minutes about the hopeless state of things. Voice is power, and poetry gives us back our voice.

Poetry also continues to do its heavy lifting through sound, rhythm, and overall musicality, which in a written form often play out in line and stanza breaks and length. We tend to read short lines and stanzas slowly and long lines faster, and our eyes tend to land more on beginning and ending words, so I often tell students that the first and last words in a poem, a stanza, and a line tend to weigh more than what's in between. The sounds of the words catalyze their own resonance. Consider many curse words with all their hard and clipped sounds compared to lullaby words which often sound softer. Each word is a vehicle for tone and, put together, the words create their own rhythm. In fact, all language has its own rhythm (you would clap out the rhythm of this sentence right now), but in poetry, we pay special attention to music.

All is all, poetry is the embodiment of a small change since it innately tilts language a little differently than how we normally encounter words so that we can shift our perspective toward new, ancient, or expanded horizons. Anyone who's taken poetry writing workshops or read a lot of poems probably already knows that a good poem offers, above all, fresh, original language that helps us to see big or small things in new ways. Along the way, we see our interconnected experiences, such as in Joy Harjo's "A Map the Next World," in which she writes, "For the soul is a wanderer with many hands and feet."

As many hands and feet wandering this earth, we can find on the path of poetry just how interconnected we are. According to physicists, we only need look at "The Butterfly Effect," in which, although it might take a long time, a butterfly flapping its wings in New Mexico could actually cause a hurricane in China. We are integral parts (and often major disruptors) of our ecosystem, but also of our human communities from how one gesture, word, deed, or mishap can cause everything from minor misunderstandings to major chaos within our families, friend circles, and communities. Poetry, in showing us how to see a path between the ordinary to what else is or isn't in plain sight, illuminates our interconnections and the power of our actions.

Peripheral vision is one of the greatest gifts of poetry, teaching us to look beyond our habitual gaze. Poetry's specific, sensory images that invite in our whole selves, and its musicality that matches the essence of the poem's rhythm with our own heartbeat, makes what's under the surface more visible while also illuminating the visible all around us. Adrienne Rich writes in "An Atlas of the Difficult World" of an abused woman, and then tells us how she doesn't want to know "wreckage, dreck, and waste, but these are the materials...." reminding us that the path to any real change in the world depends on opening our eyes to the destructive forces in our world. Yet she also reminds us that "the materials" are also the moon rising over such materials along with "... wild tree frogs calling in/ another season, light and music still pouring over/ our fissured, cracked terrain." In this excerpt, she shows us both what's often hidden and always visible, calling on us to look openly at the pain of the world but also at the beauty and motion on the peripheral horizon of that pain, offering us new opportunities for, if not always healing and wholeness, at least greater understanding.

Poetry teaches us, in new and renewed ways, how to see and interact with the world we live in, and recognize that we're in good company, human and otherwise. Constantly opening up our perception to see beyond our preconceived notions of reality, poetry leads us to a continuous spectrum of learning. We learn that the world is not black and white, and furthermore, composed of a myriad of textures and shapes, all in motion. We learn that humans are far more complex than we imagined, even and especially ourselves. We learn that life is always changing and evolving, often without our consent and outside of our plans.

So, what does any of this have to do with peace? We foster peace, in part, by opening our eyes to a wider and deeper view of the world, and in essence, waking up to both the stark realities of trauma, poverty, war—and other violence—that are sometimes fueled by the misconception that we are separate from one another. "For it is important that awake people be awake," William Stafford tells us in his poem, "A Ritual to Read to One Another" before reminding us to give clear signals to those around us because "the darkness around us is deep." A poem can give us an expanded ability to see clearly not just what's wounded and wanting, but what possibilities we have for Tikkun Olam, the Hebrew calling for us all to fix the broken world.

What do we do with the pain and suffering we witness? There's no truer old cliché than "Peace begins with me." The way we work with our feelings of groundlessness, confusion, grief, anger, and insecurity have a constant and direct impact on the peace we do or don't cultivate in our lives and the lives around us. Wendell Berry reminds us how that peace may begin with us, but it's inherently our intersection with the world that makes and keep us. In "The Peace of Wild Things," he tells of resting in this peace: "I come into the presence of still water. / And I feel above me the day-blind stars/ waiting for their light."

"Peace at the Crossroads"
A Poem and Story

When I was asked to write a poem for Peace at the Crossroads, an event organized by the American Friends Service Committee and held in Kansas City in November of 2010, I started with the peace available to us in each breath, a way to inhale and exhale, staying with wherever we are at the moment, and how each breath is an arrival at a particular intersection of time and place, personal history and world events, the emotional weather coloring how we see the world and the economic, social and artistic weather of the world-at-large. I wanted to show readers and listeners how peace is available in simply staying with whatever we feel, what struggles we face, what critical moments scare or hurt us, what possibilities abound also. Arriving in peace so often means not departing for other distractions, such as turning the anxiety of being present with the hard moments into the distractions of aggression toward ourselves or others.

Pema Chodron, a well-known Tibetan Buddhist nun, writes wisely about this seemingly simple but lifelong lesson of how to stay with what comes. Staying means getting very familiar with our habitual responses to feeling threatened by loss and pain. By understanding how we churn our fear and anxiety into limiting or even hurting ourselves, and silencing or avoiding others, we can better locate the pause button between pain and action. Once we learn to pause in that intersection, we have the opportunity to consider how to move, speak and be in the world in a way that fosters greater peace in our lives and the lives around us.

Life often gives us multiple opportunities to learn this. Not so surprisingly, the evening I went to the Crossroads district of Kansas City, Missouri to read this poem at the small festival, held in a vacant lot between two buildings, I had to make my way through massive crowds racing through the area for the art walk and local bars. By the time I got to the stage to read, the noise was deafening, a little from the little "Peace at the Crossroads" festival, and a lot from hundreds of people laughing or yelling. I was grateful to have both a mic and an audience of a dozen people ready to listen. But after I read this poem, and began to make up an improvised poem about peace, a marching band of eight people dressed up as bears, giraffes, and elephants, spilled over from the art walk and made its way loudly right in front of me. What I was going to say dissipated. The audience, caught between craning their necks to see where the marching animals went with their toy xylophones and drums, waited to hear what would happen next. Rather than go with the flash of anger from trying to make up poetry in a place whirling with so many other distractions, I took a breath, then said, "In the middle of the poem, the marching animal band comes and tells us to look around. Anything can happen at any moment. And it does."

Peace is at the intersections, as are humor and ease. Peace starts with us taking whatever material life gives us, and staying with those materials long enough to learn what to do with them.

The Crossroads in Every Step

We breathe in intersections, taking in here,
exhaling there: memory and physiology,
myth and heartwood, daring leap and long sleep.
Peace spreads itself into a recognizable shape—
leaves, the sky between, and mostly the falling
that feeds the base of this tree, the start of another.
The world is made of glimmer and tatters,
the light left by one for another, the dull shine
of mid-afternoon on the driveway gravel,
the iridescent car's reflection in the side-view mirror.

No place that isn't an intersection: you're born out of
two people's meeting, you die by at another crossroads.
No center that's not edge, no time that's not all times,
what you've lived petaling out, what you're living
rooting down, what you may live over the eastern
horizon,
a kind of weather that might organize itself into a storm
or fall apart as the blue sky bleeds through.
No matter what happens, the air will be different.

The dragonfly lands on your palm or not.
Nothing ever to hold but this need for holding.
You think you're moving through, but actually
the convergence is moving you.

References

Aristotle. (1997) *Poetics*. Translated by Malcolm Heath. New York: Penguin.

Berry, W. (1999) *The Selected Poems of Wendell Berry*. New York: Counterpoint.

Chodron, P. (1997) *When Things Fall Apart: Heart Advice for Difficult Times*. Boulder, CO: Shambhala.

Goldberg, N. (2016) *Writing Down the Bones: Freeing the Writer Within*. Boulder, CO: Shambhala.

Mirriam-Goldberg, C. & Locke, S. (2014) "The Crossroads in Every Step." *Chasing Weather: Tornadoes, Tempests, and Thunderous Skies in Word and Image* Iowa City, IA: Ice Cube Press.

Rich, A. (1991) *An Atlas of the Difficult World: Poems 1998-91*. New York: W.W. Norton.

Stafford, W. "A Ritual to Read to Each Other." *Poetry Foundation*. https://www.poetryfoundation.org/poems/58264/a-ritual-to-read-to-each-other. Accessed July 22, 2017.

Williams, W. C. "William Carlos Williams 101." *Poetry Foundation*. https://www.poetryfoundation.org/articles/92531/william-carlos-williams-101-58a72eec11bed.%20Accessed%20July%2022,%20 2017

Chapter Ten

Wisdom of the Ancestors: In Memory of Brother Blue— The Butterfly Man

Mama Linda Goss

O, Great Ancestral Storyteller,
Brother Blue,
Whispers in our ears
The journey of the Butterfly:
"Aaaaaaaaaaaaaaaaaaaaah!"
So we the Story Weavers
May spread our wings
And uplift the Listeners
To Fly Over the Rainbow
And Dip their Souls
Into the Golden Pond
OF IMAGINATION.

NOTES

© 2017 by Linda Goss
Printed with permission of Linda Goss, generously given in March 2017.
See "The Strength of Butterflies" in Part 2: Work

Part Two
Work

WORK

"Engagement in mental or physical activity as a means
to fulfill a purpose or achieve a result."
—Lyn Ford

"ACTIONS SPEAK LOUDER THAN WORDS." ISN'T THAT THE OLD ADAGE?
And sometimes words can be very loud. Any broadcast of opinion
pieces, reality programs, or political debates reminds us of that.

For our actions to speak even louder, to impact those around
us more than the rhetoric of prejudices, privilege, and panic, requires
effort, sometimes struggle, always determination. That effort may
never be recognized, but its impact may begin a ripple effect across
the surface of our world, a current that can become a wave of change.
Storytelling and the inclusion of storytelling in one's work can be a
drop of activism that can generate a ripple.

The articles and stories included in this part reveal lessons,
actions, and lives that formed works of heart, guiding participants
toward peaceful possibilities.

Chapter Eleven

First Steps Toward Peace: Building Empathy

Sherry Norfolk

> You've got to be taught
> To hate and fear,
> You've got to be taught
> From year to year,
> It's got to be drummed
> In your dear little ear
> You've got to be carefully taught.
> —Oscar Hammerstein, *South Pacific*

WHERE DO WE BEGIN—WHEN DO WE BEGIN—to teach children the *opposite* of hate and fear? When do we begin to work towards peace?

We have to begin as early as possible, teaching children empathy, compassion, acceptance, and nonviolent conflict resolution skills from an early age.

How? Through story!

Michele Borba, author of *UnSelfie: Why Empathetic Kids Succeed in Our All-About-Me World*, encourages adults to help kids build their *empathy muscles* through play-acting, reading books that let them get inside characters' minds. Stories are opportunities for kids to practice perspective-taking skills. What do the characters think, believe, want, or feel? And how do we know it?

"The right book can stir a child's empathy better than any lesson or lecture ever could," writes Borba.

The right story matched with the right child can be the gateway to opening his heart to humanity—to peace.

In fact, "… storytelling and reading stories to children should be primary instructional strategies" for teaching empathy, compassion, and nonviolence." (Vessels, 1998)

When children listen to stories, they identify with the characters—they empathize. Every time I tell Linda Goss's wonderful story, "The Frog Who Wanted to be a Singer," I see this in action. The story is about a little frog who is a frustrated singer because only the birds are allowed to sing. Finally, Little Frog gets up the courage to sing in front of all the animals, but when he faces them his courage fails. He goes offstage disheartened.

The audience is disheartened as well: long faces and huge, sad eyes characterize every face. Then Little Frog returns to the stage —but it takes a few tries before his voice cooperates. The children are on the edges of their seats, anxious and aching for Little Frog to sing—and then, he does! Bodies relax, children sigh in relief and smiles break out throughout the audience.

This story helps develop empathy muscles: the ability to understand and share another person's experiences and emotions.

Listening to stories sets young listeners free to identify with the characters' experiences and share their emotions—it allows them to "get inside" the characters' minds and helps them understand *why* they do *what* they do.

To take it a step further, provide children with the opportunity to act out the stories—to *inhabit* and *embody* the characters.

Try this activity, inspired by Lyn Ford in her Master Class at the 2016 National Storytelling Conference. The step-by-step approach layers language on top of sensory experience and physical activity, allowing children to process the actions and feelings of the characters in multiple modalities:

Step One

Discuss how movement and posture can help listeners understand the feelings and actions in a story.

Exercise—Give each child a slip of paper with a "secret" action on it (if children are not reading yet, simply whisper the action in their ears). Some suggestions:

- Kick a soccer ball
- Lick an ice cream cone
- Blow up a balloon
- Pet a big dog
- Carry a stack of books
- Open a birthday present

One at a time, children stand in front of the group and silently demonstrate their action; the audience tries to guess what they are doing. Emphasize that showing emotion (fear of the dog, excitement at opening a present) helps us understand the action.

Step Two

Now, tell a simple two-character story such as "How the Chipmunk Got Its Stripes." Many Aesop fables work for this activity too, for example "The Lion and the Mouse". Explain that pairs of children will be retelling the story with *no words*. In telling the story, try to refrain from using actions yourself, providing a blank slate for the kids.

How the Chipmunk Got Its Stripes
A Mongolian folktale, retold by Sherry Norfolk

Old Bear woke up from his long winter nap. He was very hungry—time to get up!

Bear tried to stand up, but he was so weak from hunger and old age that he could barely move. He finally managed to crawl painfully out of his cave, but couldn't go any further. He laid in the spring sunshine, panting and moaning.

Chipmunk came along, on his way to gather some of the food he had stored away last fall. He saw Old Bear lying there.

"Good morning, Old Bear. Did you have a nice nap?" Chipmunk asked.

In answer, the bear simply groaned. Chipmunk came closer.

"Are you sick, old Bear? Can I help you?"

"I'm very hungry, Chipmunk, but I'm too old and weak to hunt for food. I'm going to die," answered the bear sadly.

"Oh, no! Don't give up – maybe I can help you!" Chipmunk said. He hurried off and dug up some of the nuts that he had buried last fall, then ran back to the bear.

"Try these!" Old Bear took the nuts gratefully and crunched them. As soon as Chipmunk saw how much Old Bear liked the nuts, he continued to find and dig up as many nuts as he could, offering them to the bear.

"Are you feeling better, Old Bear?" Chipmunk asked.

Old Bear stretched and began to stand. "Yes, Chipmunk, thanks to you, I feel much better. I'm strong enough to hunt for food myself now. Thank you, my friend."

Bear reached out to hug little Chipmunk in thanks, softly stroking Chipmunk's back. Even though he was very gentle, his claws made lines on Chipmunk's back that we can still see today. They remind us of Chipmunk's kindness and generosity.

Discussion:

- How did Old Bear feel at the beginning of the story? Why?
- How did Chipmunk feel when Old Bear told him he was dying? Why?
- How did Old Bear feel when Chipmunk brought him food? Why?
- How did Chipmunk feel when Old Bear was able to stand up? Why?
- How will these two animals feel about each other from now on? How will they act towards each other?
- How can you use your face and body to show how the characters feel?

Exercise: Pair up the children, explaining that one will be Old Bear and one will be Chipmunk. Instruct them to practice telling the story with no words, only actions. Allow time for partners to switch roles so that each has a chance to experience the story from both perspectives. Circulate among the pairs, reminding them that they need to show not only what the characters are doing, but how they feel.

Ask each pair to silently act out their version of the story for the class. Afterward, discuss how body language and facial expression helped the audience understand what the characters were doing and how the characters were feeling.

Step Three

Discuss how sounds can help interpret a story.

Exercise:

Give each child a slip of paper with a "sound" named on it (if children are not reading yet, simply whisper in their ears). Some suggestions:

- Bouncing on bed
- Jumping into water
- Slurping ice cream
- Dog whining
- Cracking an egg
- Wind blowing

One at a time, children stand in front of the group and make their sound; the audience tries to guess what sound they are making. Most children will also act it out—that's okay! Emphasize that showing emotion (such as excited bouncing, sad dog) helps us to interpret the sound.

In the same pairs, instruct children to practice telling the story with actions *and sound effects*—still using no words. Allow time for partners to switch roles so that each has a chance to experience the story from both perspectives.

Ask each pair to present their version of the story for the class. Afterward, discuss how body language, facial expression, and sounds helped the audience understand what the characters were doing and how the characters were feeling.

Step Four

Now it's time to add the words. By now, the children empathize deeply with the characters and have a clear understanding of the story structure. Layering language on top of their sensory experiences and physical actions will prove fairly easy.

Discussion: What information was not conveyed through the actions and sounds? Who should be the narrator? What information can the narrator add to the actions and sounds? How can words help the audience better understand what is happening?

Point out that the characters can now use their voices to *talk* to each other. What kind of voices should they have? Will they sound happy or sad or concerned or cheerful, etc.?

Group Exercise: Tell the children that they will be the actors and you will be the director. The only word that they will

say is "Oh"—but you will be telling them how to say the word, for example:
- As if you are smelling a dirty diaper
- As if you just received a million dollars
- As if you are seeing a ghost
- As if you are very bored
- As if you are looking at a cute puppy

Discuss how the feeling behind the word changes the way it sounds.

Pairs practice again, telling the story with actions, sound effects, narration, conversation, and vocal expression. Allow time for partners to switch roles so that each has a chance to experience the story from both perspectives, and each has been the narrator. Circulate, encouraging the characters to speak expressively.

Ask each pair to present their version of the story for the class. Follow with some character interviews:
- Old Bear, how did you feel about chipmunks and other small animals before this happened to you? Why?
- Chipmunk, how did you feel about bears and other big creatures before this happened? Why?
- Old Bear, did you believe that a little chipmunk could help you? Why or why not?
- Chipmunk, you gave all your food to Old Bear. What will you do now?
- Chipmunk and Bear, how have your feelings about each other changed? Why?
- If a chipmunk and a bear can learn to be friends, perhaps we can learn to be friends with people who are very different from us.

∞

This lesson may be a first step towards developing *empathy muscles*—a first step towards peace.

They've got to be carefully taught.

Notes & References

All of these exercises—and many more!—are fully delineated in *Children Tell Stories: Teaching and Using Storytelling in the Classroom* (2nd ed.) by Martha Hamilton and Mitch Weiss (Richard C. Owen Publishers, 2005)

Borba, M. (2016) *UnSelfie: Why Empathetic Kids Succeed in Our All-About-Me World*. New York: Touchstone.

Commonsense Media. *Books that Teach Empathy*. https://www. commonsensemedia.org/lists/books-that-teach-empathy#

Goss, L. (1996) *The Frog Who Wanted to be a Singer*. New York: Orchard Books.

Taletellerin's blog. "How the Chipmunk Got Its Stripes." https:// taletellerin.wordpress.com/2010/04/23/8-the-chipmunks-stripes/

Tinybop. *13 Kids Books to Spark Empathy*. https://tinybop.com/ blog/13-books-to-spark-conversations-about-empathy

Vessels, G.G. (1998) *Character and Community Development: A School Planning and Teacher Training Handbook*. Westport, CT: Praeger.

Chapter Twelve

"… So That My Story Takes a Happy Ending"

Storytelling in "Willkommensklassen"
Kristin Wardetzky

"Alone we can do so little, together we can do so much."
—Helen Keller

HANNAH ARENDT WRITES IN HER ESSAY "WE REFUGEES" in 1943 about the destiny of Jewish refugees and others:

> We have lost our homes, that is the ordinariness of
> everyday life. We have lost our jobs, that is the trust
> to be good for something. We have lost the ability
> to communicate, that is the spontaneous reactions,
> the simplicity of gestures, the natural expression of
> emotions, that is, our private life is broken.

Can you find a more precise, more emphatic way to outline the situation of the refugees that are currently coming to Germany than with those modest words? The immigrant, as Hannah Arendt writes, is the stranger, who has to try and orient himself in the civilization and culture of a completely foreign group, a group that should accept him or tolerate him at the very least (Arendt, S. 34).

Initially, the individual focuses—besides the protection of existential needs—on learning the language of the "destination country," which happens to be of more complexity than getting to understand words and grammar.

> For each word and each sentence can have multiple associations, which surround them with a circle of emotional values and which is different from culture to culture. Each speech element gains its special meaning, which stems from the context and the social environment (Schütz, S. 53).

Those meanings are determined by cultural and traditional codings, and they have to get decrypted, which implicitly happens through perception and interpretation of nonverbal signals—an oftentimes trigger of irritation, as well as misconception.

Based on these concepts, the members of the association "Erzählkunst e.V." reinforced their engagement in different areas of charity work for refugees. Among other things they offered the *Storytelling Arena*—a forum in which young Syrians, connected with storytellers of the association, told traditional and autobiographical stories in Arabic, German, and English, accompanied by music, songs, and dances. Other storytellers invited families to storytelling events, just as they cooked and told stories together with women who fled from their home countries. In conjunction with those and other events, the first care was for children and teenagers. Due to the long-time experience of storytelling in schools of inner city districts, they were aware that storytelling could provide access to the German language, which, as described earlier, opens culturally-embossed *Sinnhorizonte,* horizons of meaning, thus conveying verbal and gestural codings and allowing language become a bridge to emotion and imagination. The storytellers conducted six *Willkommensklassen* in two schools in Berlin from January to July 2016.

However, despite their social competence with students and

toddlers, the encounters were extremely challenging at first. Most students had little or no knowledge of the German language at all. They originated from foreign cultures, had dealt with the experience of escape and war, and a majority were living under the depressing conditions of refugee camps.

How does one tell those children and teenagers a fairytale? How do you make such stories relevant to the children? How do you get those children to listen, how do you reach their imagination, but especially their emotional sympathy? How do you motivate them to tell stories themselves, even in broken German?

What happened in the schools from January to July is truly impressive: The six-to-nine-year-olds quickly developed a ritualized schedule concerning the storytelling sessions: Each weekly session started with the same song, which was easy for children to remember, and which they sang with huge excitement. Signs of tiring of the song were not visible. Next, every child presented a picture that he or she had drawn individually in class after last week's story. Classmates' applause made faces glow with pride. Along with the storyteller, the children left reality with a rhyming language game and made their way to the land of fairytales. The doorway to fairyland only opened after they had solved three riddles. While in the beginning those riddles were provided by the storytellers, after a short while the children excelled, regaling each other with, as it seemed, unsolvable riddles.

The main part of each session was the actual storytelling. At first, the storytellers relied on trans-lingual signals along with talking, to help listeners to remain attentive and understand the language beyond the mere expression of words, substantially distinguishing the live storytelling from listening to audiovisual media, a factor that is of elementary significance for the children.

> Language and speech develop in a dialogical situation,
> in which it is essential to listen, to copy and to come
> into contact. Children learn a language especially in a

situation where people listen to one another carefully and where they have the possibility to listen without interruptions (Glück-Levi, S. 489).

Furthermore, the storytellers increasingly used graphic material—mostly images in Kamishibai—which illustrated the storyline, along with natural materials and other illustrative objects. Thus, despite verbal gaps, the children were able to understand the stories—initially only roughly, but little by little even in detail. A huge increase in comprehension was visible, as seen in the pictures they drew afterward.

Even with this description, it is hard to create an accurate impression of the excitement with which the children entered the *Storytelling Room*, an additional classroom provided by the schools. How joyfully they listened week by week, to the chanted rhymes. How breathlessly they followed the fairytales. They occasionally burst into exuberant laughter, or—during the last weeks—even warned the hero of the story of upcoming danger or imprudent actions by verbal remarks. The intensity of their concentration and the eruptive joy that seemed to fill their entire bodies, made their faces light up in beauty—those were the moments that held their very own magic.

One of the educators, who, (along with the teachers), participated in the storytelling sessions, claimed she had never seen the children as lively as during the fairytales. Lively—yes, sometimes they were very excited—though at the same time completely at peace with themselves. Lively—in all their childlike impartiality and integrity.

On the other hand, the children experienced an irreplaceable form of self-acknowledgment by becoming part of the storytelling, despite their lack of German words and phrases. They translated the gestures of the storytellers into pictures in their head and fill the gaps of comprehension with material of their own associative memory—a profound mental task that strengthens and expands imaginative and intellectual competencies. During the telling, they experienced language differently than in educational contexts or their daily life.

Even children who possessed little to no knowledge of the German language followed the "signals" of the storyteller with unhindered concentration. Language—just as the gestures and mime of the storyteller—transformed into pictorial associations, triggering emotions or predictions. The plain comprehension of vocabulary became a visualization of characters, setting, and action, development of affective sympathy, interpretation, and enjoyment.

H. G. Gadamer explains in a different context that this gain of linguistic skills has been proved by various storytelling projects to "… result from the gradual understanding of the conventions of a language, […] which does not consist of a rigid system of rules of the schoolmasters, but in the flexible agreement of those who speak with each other (Gadamer, S. 11).

The project in the Hildebrandt school will be continued next school year. This time, an additional involvement of the parents is planned. We are hoping this will result in the parents telling stories from their home countries, while the children operate as interpreters.

Working with fourteen-to-eighteen-year-olds demanded different skills from the storytellers. This time they managed to find a generative balance between their experiences with both theatre pedagogy and storytelling. Thus, Christine Lander writes in her final report:

> Along with other things, the students conducted partner interviews, drafted stories in self-drawn pictures and improvised on stage. Every one of them had outlined their body shape on a piece of paper that he or she filled with symbols of his or her biographical story. By the aid of those pictures, the message that everyone is filled with stories was successfully conveyed. Even the teenagers that initially claimed they had nothing to tell, soon excitingly started to search for stories. Eventually, every student had settled on a story they found worthy to continue working on. […] During the second phase of

the project, the stories were written down and, encouraged by teachers and group leaders, revised in content and language. First, the teenagers started practicing to tell their stories freely in small groups, soon bigger ones and in the end in front of a camera and the entire class. Furthermore, anyone who had the desire could even present their story to a bigger audience of three other classes. As medial results of the project, the story videos of the students, a video documentary and pictures can be named."

After initially hesitating, the students started to remember more and more stories from their home countries: Syria, Iraq, Iran, Afghanistan, Somalia, Kosovo, and so on. The majority consisted of "wisdom stories" with oftentimes a funny or philosophical punch line. Here we have two examples:

The Tale of a Turtle

A little turtle walks into the forest and sees how fast the rabbits can run. Oh, it thinks, I want to be just as fast as them! It asks the animals what it could do to become as fast as them. However, the rabbits tell it that the house it is carrying on its back will be too heavy – the turtle could never win a running competition with it. Deeply saddened, the turtle walks home and tells its mother about its sorrows:

"I won't ever be able to run fast because my house is too heavy!"

The mother answers, "The house will protect you from the sun and danger!"

"Yes, but it is too heavy!" replies the little turtle.

"Yes, that is life—it is too heavy," says the mother.

Guha and His Friends

Guha owns nothing except for a sheep which he loves more than anything else in the world. Wherever he goes, the sheep will accompany him. One day, his friends want to slaughter and eat it, though Guha does not want to give it to them. His friends convince him by claiming the world would be ending the next day and he would not need the sheep anymore. Thus, Guha gives them the sheep and they slaughter and eat it.

The next morning, Guha takes all his friends' clothes and burns them. As they wake up and ask him why he did that, he answers: "You said the world was ending today. You won't need your clothes anymore!"

It seems likely that the students, and refugees in general, hold way more of those treasures or are willing to quickly look them up on their phone. Without being aware of it, they come to our country with immaterial treasures. Those treasures let the buzzword "diversity" become a sensual experience and convey a foreshadow of the expansion of our cultural horizons that we can expect from those certain encounters.

Additionally, the project showed that the phrase "Storytelling creates community" is not a meaningless sentence. It was truly touching to witness the teenagers supporting each other throughout the process of telling, helping one another when they were lacking German words, or looking up phrases and equivalents from their mother tongue on their phones. The students were bonded together by the invisible tie of storytelling, which made feelings of foreignness and isolation vanish unexpectedly fast.

Creating their safe space in a community which was supportive, attentive and affectionate, the students became storytellers themselves, which made them experience an irreplaceable form of self-confirmation.

One of the most impressive experiences regarding the work with the teenagers was their sudden openness with which they sometimes started telling details about their escape, even without a demand. You could barely hear breathing in the silence that arose afterward. What evidence of trust towards the storytellers. What a sign that storytelling starts to clear the tight netting of memory. Almost physically perceptible was the feeling of community in those moments. Looking in the teenagers' faces, you could tell that they were friends with both themselves and the others. It was not about having to prove oneself or recognition, but about being understood, by oneself and by others. It was about being friends—with oneself and the others.

The future of the project with the teenagers is still uncertain due to funding. If we can keep working on it, our goal is to motivate the students to tell stories in the "Willkommensklassen" of the six-to-nine-year-olds by the end of the year.

If we manage to continue the project, the mutual exchange, the dialogue, the mutual communication about disconnections and relations [...] something new, something unexpected can develop (Wagner, S. 245).

By this, the term *interculturality* gains a sensual resonance of respect, attention, and curiosity towards the stranger—the stranger on both sides!

Hence, it is not about one-sided adaptation (of the refugees) to the deeply rooted lifestyle of a norm group, or about an adjustment of norms, but about the mutual commitment that provides the willingness to change on both sides. Even considering all the difficulties connected to such transformational processes, we should not forget that our own culture developed its profile only by being in constant exchange with other cultures: The *minnesongs* (songs of courtly love, from the Mid-19th century), Goethe's "West-Eastern Divan," Grimm's collection of fairytales, Brecht's epic theatre—all of them are not imaginable without the influence of other cultures.

Cultures always developed in a mutual penetration [dissemination] of different influences. [...] Culture is always "between the cultures" (Alexander Düttmann), it is never 'pure' and homogeny, but hybrid, a 'Bastard' (ebd., S. 249).

My point is: By working with refugees we, ourselves, will change as well. How I wish the media would not constantly focus on the cost of the refugee policy or the fear of terror, but rather take the infinite multiplicity of examples, in which participation is being lived, not only claimed, and in which the exchange with other cultures is an infusing substance and source of inspiration that helps experience energetic potential.

Personally, I find those projects, which I accompanied voluntarily, to be some of the most important and touching experiences of my entire life.

Notes & References

Willkommensklassen are special separate classes in mainstream schools, established to prepare non-German students to further their educations through German language acquisition.

This article was posted at http://www.fest-network.eu on May 29, 2017. Reprinted with generous permission from the author, Dr. Kristin Wardetzky, and with the kind assistance of Sonia Carmona Tapia, Cultural Agent and Theatre Director for Aaiun Producciones, who posted the article at the FEST blog (Federation of European Storytelling).

Dr. Wardetzky's article was translated into English by her granddaughter, Lea Hauser.

Arendt, H. (1943/2015) Wir Flüchtlinge ("We Refugees"). In Langenohl, Poole, A. & Weinberg, R. (Hg.): *Transkulturalität*. Klassische Texte. Bielefeld, S. 33–44.

Gadamer, H.G. (1998) Unterwegs zur Schrift? ("On the Road to Writing")
In Assmann, A., Assmann, & Hardmeier, C. (Hg.): *Schrift und
Gedächtnis*. Archäologie der literarischen Kommunikation.
München. S. 10–19.

Glück-Levi, M. (2012) Hören und Sprechen lernen. In Bockhorst, H.,
Reinwand,V.-I. & Zacharias, W. (Hg.): *Handbuch Kulturelle
Bildung*. München, S. 488–490.

Schütz, A. (1944/2015): Der Fremde. Ein sozialpsychologischer Versuch.
In Langenohl, A., Poole, R. & Weinberg, M.(Hg.): *Transkulturalität*.
Klassische Texte. Bielefeld, S. 45–59.

Wagner, B. (2012) Von der Multikultur zur Diversität "From
Multiculturalism to Diversity"). In Bockhorst, H., Reinwand,
V.-I. & Zacharias, W.: *Handbuch Kulturelle Bildung*. München, S.
245-251.

Chapter Thirteen

The Queen Bee: A Grimm's Tale
Starting the Year Off Right in Kindergarten
By Jane Stenson

"I invite everyone to choose forgiveness rather than division,
teamwork over personal ambition."
—Jean-Francois Cope

KINDERGARTEN IS THE BEGINNING OF SCHOOLING for many children, and we want to start them off right! We need to help young children regard their classmates as friends with whom they will spend the year; to help egocentric children develop a sense of themselves as cooperative, caring members of a group; and to develop listening skills. It's important for the teacher to be forthright about her expectations about behavior, and to embed peaceful conflict resolution into our daily school lives.

At the beginning of the school year (in fact, the second day of school) I, the teacher, tell the story "The Queen Bee" to my kindergarten class because I want to give children the opportunity to be their best selves; I want to tell them that this is the behavior I expect in school. I want to give us (children and teacher) a shared experience and shared language to talk about how we treat each other;

so, telling "The Queen Bee" is my first step in teaching pro-active conflict resolution procedures. I also want to begin teaching narrative structure and this story's structure is abundantly clear. It also contains vocabulary that five- and six-year-olds will have to determine through context.

The hero who is the third son is filled with compassion for living things—his father, his brothers, the creatures of the earth, sea, and air, and the people he meets. It is his compassion or caring that guides him to be fair and honest, to be responsible and to act as a good citizen in the enchanted place he and his brothers enter. He cares and therefore acts so deeply that the land "where there was nothing that was not stone" is restored or transformed by his actions to life in the fields and the manor house and in relationships.

The Queen Bee
A Grimm's tale retold by Jane Stenson

Once upon a time, there lived a man with three sons. The two eldest were spendthrifts and n'er-do-wells. They frittered away their time and squandered their money. The youngest son was hardworking and cheerful.

One day the two older boys went to their father and said, "We are going out into the world to seek our fortune." Their father wished them well and off they went. The father was happy to be with his youngest son because they accomplished much and were pleased with each other. But after a time, the son said to his father that he too wished to go out into the world, find his brothers, and seek his fortune. The father didn't want him to go, but he gave his son his blessing, wished him well, and off the lad went.

Soon he met up with his brothers who said, "What are you doing here?" The youngest brother replied that he wanted to join them and make his way in the world and seek his fortune. The older brothers laughed and laughed and said, "We who are older haven't found our fortune yet, what makes you think you can find yours?"

"Nevertheless," said the youngest, "I would like to try." So they all walked on together.

They came to an anthill. All the ants were busy working. "Say," said the oldest brother, "Let's scruff up these anthills and kill all the ants!"

"No," said the youngest, "The ants have done us no harm. We must leave them alone."

"Oh no, you're no fun," said the eldest brother.

The three walked on and soon came to a lake where many ducks were swimming. "Oooo, look at that!" said the older boys, "We're really hungry. Let's shoot some of those ducks and roast them for our dinner."

"No!" said the youngest, "They have done us no harm. We must leave them alone."

"Here we go again," said the older boys.

They continued walking and espied a tree with honey oozing down the side and a large beehive in its boughs. "Ah!" said the older brothers. "Let's build a fire at the base of the tree and smoke out those bees."

"No!" said the youngest brother, "The bees have done us no harm. Leave them alone."

"That's enough!" said the older brothers They were disgusted. "You better decide if you're coming with us or if you should go home. You are no fun at all."

On the three of them walked until, after a while, they came to a large manor house surrounded by fields. The house was completely made out of stone. *Everything* on the outside was made of stone: the grass, the trees, the fields, the sheep, the cows. There was nothing that was not stone.

The brothers walked to the front door and knocked. When no one answered, they opened the door and went in. Everything on the inside was made of stone: the drapes, the tables, the chairs, the light fixtures, the rug, even the cookies on the plate. There was nothing that was not stone.

They walked through every part of the manor house until they came to a closed wooden door at the back of the house. They knocked lightly and opened the door. Inside the room was an old man seated at a table. He asked them what they wanted.

The brothers said, "We have come to seek our fortune."

"Well," said the old man, "You may have come to the right place. You see, I used to be a king. Many years ago, a spell was placed on this castle. Everything was turned to stone except for me and my three daughters. If you can accomplish three tasks between sunup and sundown, you can break the magic spell. If you succeed, you will inherit half of my property and may marry one of my daughters. However, if you fail any task, you too will be turned to stone."

"Oh, I would surely like to try!" said the eldest brother.

The next morning at sunup the oldest brother was given the first task: to find one thousand pearls that had been scattered about the castle grounds. The brother searched all day, and by sundown, he had found only two hundred pearls. He was instantly turned to stone.

On the next day, the middle brother searched and he found only five hundred pearls. He was turned to stone.

On the third morning, the youngest brother went to the front steps of the manor house and sat on the steps. He put his head in his hands and a tear slid down his cheek. The queen of the ants went to him and asked him why he was crying.

"Because I have to find 1,000 pearls by sundown or I will be turned to stone. My older brothers tried and failed and I don't see how I can accomplish the task. I don't think I can break the spell."

The queen of the ants said, "You saved our lives and now, we'll save yours." All the ants went throughout the grounds gathering pearls and gave them to the youngest brother who gave them to the old man.

The next morning the old man met the boy on the bank of the lake. "My king's ring was thrown out into the lake by the Enchantress and you must find it by sundown or you will be turned to stone." The boy did not know what to do.

Just then, the king of the ducks saw his difficulty and swam to him. The king of the ducks said, "You saved our lives and now we'll save yours." The ducks dove to the bottom of the lake and dove to the bottom of the lake. It took all day. Just as the sun was beginning to set, a duck rose to the surface and gave it to the youngest son who gave it to the king who put it on his finger.

On the third day, the youngest son entered the king's room for the third and final task.

"Stop there at the door," said the king who was seated with his three daughters who looked exactly alike. "On the lips of one of my daughters is a drop of syrup. On the lips of another is a drop of sugar water. And, the other has a drop of honey on her lips. Stand in the doorway and choose which princess has a drop of honey on her lips. Remember, if you accomplish this task, you will inherit half of my kingdom and may marry one of my daughters. If you fail you will be turned into stone."

The young man had no idea which princess had honey on her lips, but just then through an open window flew the queen bee. She flew straight to the daughter with the honey and alighted on her lip. The youngest son identified her and the spell was broken!

Everything was returned to its natural form: the sheep, the grass, the trees, the chairs and tables, even the cookies on the plate. His brothers came alive. In due course, the youngest brother married the princess with the sweet honey on her lips and they all lived happily ever after.

Week One

First Day of school: This little poem hangs on chart paper behind the teacher's chair for all to see/read it:

Hurt No Living Thing
Christina Rosetti

Hurt no living thing:
Ladybird, nor butterfly,
Nor moth with dusty wing.
Nor cricket chirping cheerily,
Nor grasshopper so light of leap,
No dancing gnat, nor beetle fat,
Nor harmless worms that creep.

Second Day of school: Tell the folktale "The Queen Bee."

Third Day of school: My intern and I get inside the puppet theatre (an old-style, emptied TV console) (very funny for the children to have the teachers on their knees doing a puppet show) with paper puppets taped on craft sticks and tell the story on our knees while the children watch the puppet show as if they were watching TV. I know by now that they know the story and can tell it. In fact, when we say the words a bit differently, some children correct us! I want that flexibility to be part of our lives together as well.

Fourth Day of School: Discuss the story: What did you like? What happened? Do you think there was a real place where there was nothing that was not stone? What is the story about? I accept every answer.

Fifth Day of School: Choose six children to create a kindergarten-style storyboard. Using the plot and a six-frame basic storyboard format have each child draw a picture and dictate the language to "tell" the story on an 8" X 12" piece of colored paper. When completed, I cut it out in an irregular shape, glue their pictures/words to a big (24" X 36") piece of tagboard. At the *rug-time* later in the morning, the children will then tell the story to their classmates … to much applause! "What great storytellers!"

One of the picture books I read this week is *Mr. Gumpy's Outing* by John Burningham. It's about Mr. Gumpy taking many animals on a boat ride. As each asks and receives permission to get on the boat, Mr. Gumpy cautions the sheep, "Yes you may come, but no bleating," or to the goat, "Yes, you may come but no kicking," and so on with each animal. Everything proceeds smoothly for a while, but then the sheep bleats and the goat kicks, etc., until the boat tips and everyone falls in the water. Mr. Gumpy says, "Well, let's dry off; come with me and let's have some tea."

Week Two

On the playground and in the classroom by now someone has pushed or kicked or taken a block or knocked someone's work. It's important to tell children that these conflicts are a natural part of being together in a community. Some children are certain the other child "did it on purpose." Here is the opportunity to use the language of the story: "Oh, don't shoot (kick or push) him, he has done us no harm," referencing "The Queen Bee."

Conflict resolution procedures are best learned in the moment with a follow-up with the entire class. First, assuming there's no physical injury, bring the two children together calmly. One child states the offense from her point of view. The second child states the offense from his point of view. Each must listen to the other and each must look at the other. Then I ask them how to solve the problem. If they are silent, I say "Together, you created the situation, and together you two brave children can figure out the solution." I wait. Because the children want to get on with their play, they often smile at each other, offer a quick apology, and run away. But, if they need help with the language of processing the situation or if it's emotionally hard to say, "I don't like it when you … I will help them with their language. However, I will not take over the negotiation because I believe they can solve their own problems. "You created this situation together and you can solve it together."

School is a public place and being in a group, albeit a large group, means that very little is private. So, back on the rug with all the children, I often, but not always, ask the two perpetrators to tell the class what happened and how they solved the problem. My role as a teacher is to care about the children and the transaction; I accept both children and keep this conversation serious but light… because conflicts happen; they are a natural part of being together. Yes, I repeated that statement! The children need to recognize that solutions happen too, and that they can be part of the solution. This is how I build the community, two children at a time, bringing their dilemma to the entire class. The children need to understand that their concerns will be addressed at school with the teacher and with each other.

Cooperation (or how to solve problems with imagination so that every person involved can succeed and/or get his needs satisfied): Here is a math activity that helps me assess the children's counting ability as well as their styles of cooperation. It's from Creating the Peaceable School by Richard Bodine, Donna Crawford, and Fred Schrumpf. I hang a big piece of paper and print the word COOP-ERATION in the center and ask children what the word means, and to share an example of when they were cooperating with another person to accomplish a task.

I divide children into groups of three children each. Their task is to face each other and clench their fist. They shake their fist up and down counting "One, Two, Three, Four." On the count of four, each puts out any number of fingers from zero to five. Their goal is to get eleven fingers out. Each group keeps trying until they get eleven, and they may only count, and not talk, during the math play. (At a higher math level, have each group try to total twenty-three fingers, with each person using both hands.)

After most groups are successful, we talk about "What made the activity difficult?" And "What helped your group succeed?" I tell them that cooperation or working together—as well as accurate counting—are very important.

How is this working?

I return the children to "The Queen Bee" and ask them to think about cooperation, and why the animals of the land, the water, and the sky cooperated with the third son. The children's answers tell me what they have understood in the story and how they can apply it in their lives. Assessment is tricky in this regard; if a conflict happens and the children are not sophisticated in their handling of it, I reteach the procedure, and I share our common language about "Hurt no living thing" or "They have done us no harm. Leave them alone." Learning to handle conflicts and how to speak up to mediate and solve problems is a life-long quest. It needs to begin when children are young and hope is high.

REFERENCES

Bodine, R., Crawford, D. K., and Schrumpf, F. (1994) *Creating the Peaceable School: A Comprehensive Program for Teaching Conflict Resolution*. Champaign, IL: Research Press.

Burningham, J. (1970) *Mr. Gumpy's Outing*. New York: Henry Holt and Company.

Chapter Fourteen

Pathway to Peace:
Nonviolent Problem Solving

Sherry Norfolk

"... change only happens when ordinary people get involved
and they get engaged,
and they come together to demand it."
—President Barack Obama's Farewell Address, January 10,
2017

AS A STORYTELLING TEACHING ARTIST, I work in K–12 classrooms
using storytelling as a strategy for teaching curriculum. Most often,
this involves telling stories and getting kids to write by using the
pattern of the stories as the template for their own original tales. I've
been at this since 1996—that's a lot of kids and a lot of stories! One
thing I've observed over and over is that when asked to solve a story
problem, kids will often choose a violent "solution." When I explain
that violence is not an option, they always groan.

Non-violent problem-solving requires considering options and
predicting and evaluating probable outcomes. Students must learn to
brainstorm possible solutions, not just reach for the imaginary gun.

They must learn to predict the outcome of each of their possible solutions and to evaluate which of these outcomes is best. This skill does not develop automatically – like any skill, it takes practice. Storytelling and story-writing provide that practice!

Example: I tell "Wiley and the Hairy Man" with lots of character voices, sound effects, facial expression, and gestures, and we quickly establish the pattern.

- The Main Character (a kid) _____
- Is warned about Danger _____
- By an Adult character _____
- But ends up in danger anyway because _____
- He gets away WITHOUT VIOLENCE by _____

If time allows, I may tell another story that follows the same pattern, such as "Billy Brown and the Belly Button Monster" (*Boo-Tickle Tales*, 2016). After noting how the story matches the pattern, we use that pattern to generate a group story. Collaboration appears as a standard in every grade level of the Common Core Standards for English Language Arts, but taking turns and respecting one another's contributions is often problematic. We manage to agree by combining some answers and accepting others.

Then we reach the problem-solving bit. Responses typically include machine guns, bombs, knives, and poison. ("What? Poison is violent?") I point out (over and over again) that the characters in my stories used their brains rather than violence to solve their problems. Heaving huge sighs, the students finally arrive at an acceptable solution.

After I model telling the resulting story, each student uses the pattern to generate his/her own story. I circulate, noting several attempts to "solve" the problems in the stories with violence, but with only a few reminders, the stories become non-violent.

Wiley is a trickster, and trickster stories are a wonderful source of non-violent problem-solving inspiration. The little guy with no weapons except his own brains (think Br'er Rabbit, Anansi the Spider, Jack or Kantchil the Mouse Deer), is up against the big guy with the claws, teeth, and muscles (Alligator, Tiger, the Giant). The trickster uses his wits to solve the problem, but sometimes gets caught in his own cleverness. That's another lesson—lying and stealing are not clever!

I let the kids develop their own trickster character, which must meet the criteria: small, physically weak, no weapons, usually quick on his feet and always quick-witted. Here's the template:

- Name the Trickster _____
- What does the Trickster want? _____
- Why can't/won't he get it for himself? _____
- Who can he trick? _____
- What is the trick? _____
- What's the outcome? _____

Trickster tales do not lend themselves to violence. They provide a perfect opportunity for students to practice non-violent problem-solving.

For middle- and high-school students, I often begin by telling the class a Cree legend about a Skeleton Woman who first eats her own flesh and then wants to eat other humans. (Oh yes, complete engagement!)

Then I show them a collection of very ambiguous photos (super-zoom photos of bits of plants, ice formations, etc.). Up close, the photo subjects are unidentifiable and somewhat creepy. I demonstrate how to use one of these photos to create an original creepy story:

I ask one of the students to make a blind choice of one of the photos. This becomes the creepy dangerous character in our story. The students name the character, decide where it could be found, determine what it would do to a human who came in contact with it, create a voice, sounds, and movement for it, and determine how a human could defeat the creature without violence. Then I tell them their story, using their ideas plus my own addition of a protagonist who encounters the creature but gets away safely.

"Can we do it?" "I can do that—let me try!" "Let me see the rest of those pictures!" Motivation is a wonderful thing!

I spread the fifty pictures out and allow them to choose, then distribute forms with questions to help them create their character:

- The creature's name is _____
- Where does it live? _____
- What makes it dangerous? _____
- What will it do if it comes in contact with a human being?
  _____

- What kind of voice does it have? _____
- How does it move? _____
- What sounds might it make? _____
- How can it be defeated without violence? _____

The form and my instructions clearly require a non-violent solution, but it's still necessary to be vigilant. In a recent class, all but one of the stories had non-violent endings. One story simply came to a stop—no resolution at all. The listeners demanded, "So what happened to the guy? How does it end?" When the author confessed that he hadn't been able to come up with a non-violent ending, everyone spontaneously began to brainstorm solutions. He accepted one of them and finished the story.

This gave me an opportunity to deliver a very short sermon on working together to solve problems, brainstorming to discover multiple alternatives, and evaluating the options. And that resulted in the students offering new and improved endings for the stories that had already been shared!

In many of the Jack Tales, Jack is a trickster. I usually use "Jack and the King's New Ground" and "Jack and the Haunted House," pointing out the general pattern: Jack needs a job, somehow finds one, encounters an obstacle (typically a giant or witch or other magical creature), defeats the obstacle without violence, and gets rewarded.

Again, we use the pattern to generate a new story and I tell it to the class, whereupon students are asked to develop their own Jack Tale following the pattern described above. I encourage students to take their time thinking through the options and developing very creative non-violent solutions.

Learning that there are options to violence is an important step towards peaceful problem-solving. Through our story listening and story-making, kids can take a baby step in the right direction, beginning to discover their own ability to generate, evaluate and implement non-violent solutions.

Chapter Fifteen

Liz Weir: An Interview
Sherry Norfolk and Lyn Ford

"I slept and dreamt that life was joy. I awoke and saw that
life was service. I acted and behold, service was joy."
—Rabindranath Tagore

Interviewers: Hi, Liz. We appreciate your willingness to share
some of your insights and experience in this book. For those who
may not know you and your work, please tell us who you are, where
you live, and how long you have been a storyteller.

Liz: My name is Liz Weir and I live in Cushendall, County
Antrim, Northern Ireland. My home is forty miles from the city of
Belfast where I went to university and worked as Children's Librarian
for the city from 1976–1990.

I first started telling stories as a librarian forty-four years ago
and have worked full time as a storyteller for twenty-seven years.

Interviewers: What types of stories do you share? Do you
share in performance only, or as a part of keynotes, lectures, business
presentations, sermons, and other communications?

Liz: I tell mostly traditional tales from Ireland or Scotland but
also international folktales. I also lead storytelling workshops, give

lectures and participate in festivals all over the world. Corporate storytelling is another strand of my work.

Interviewers: Where do you do most of your storytelling or other work?

Liz: Like many tellers, I work in all sorts of places. I tell in schools, libraries, prisons, hospitals, and care homes. I also tell in Storytelling clubs and with various community groups including sessions for people with physical or intellectual disabilities.

Interviewers: Has your work changed over the years? If it has, when and why did you begin changing or doing your work?

Liz: My work has deepened over the years. I am now drawn more to workshops than to performance. I see myself as a "provoker" of stories, enabling people whose voices are seldom heard, for example, people with dementia, special needs or those who have undergone trauma as a result if violence in our society. I also feel I have an important role to play in the development of young story-tellers so as to leave a legacy.

Interviewers: What does the word "peace" mean to you? What is your vision of a peaceful world?

Liz: A world where people can live in harmony, valuing and respecting difference. German writer Konstantin Wecker said, "peace is when we allow ourselves to be weak." It's not all about winning, it's about admitting our own frailty and accepting the frailty of others.

Interviewers: Was there any experience in your life that pushed you to become an advocate for peace?

Liz: Having lived in Northern Ireland all my life, I have seen the destruction that violence can bring to a community. Living in a community of one and a half million people that was torn apart by violence for thirty years has made me strive to ensure a peaceful future for our children

Interviewers: Those experiences were certainly a profound catalyst! Do you consider yourself a deliberate advocate for peace, or do you consider your storytelling an organic experience for building community (either, or both)? Why? What approaches do you use?

Why and how do you think these approaches make a difference for others and in your style of storytelling?

Liz: Both! I strive to create a space where people learn to listen with respect to each other. By sharing stories, we learn to appreciate diverse viewpoints. Folktales provide a safe and yet sometimes subversive way of putting across a variety of viewpoints and often contain important non-threatening messages. I always start by working with (but not "using") traditional tales.

Interviewers: When and why did you begin to feel you were a "voice for peace"—an advocate or supporter of some effort toward bringing effective communication, comfort, social justice, or useful change into the world?

Liz: Since the early 1970s I have seen the impact that sharing stories can have within communities, be they families, schools or in our wider society.

Interviewers: Are you deliberately active in efforts toward peace at a local or regional or national or international level? If you are, tell us a little about this work.

Liz: I have been involved with many cross-community and inter-generational projects in Northern Ireland with the aim of promoting greater cultural understanding. These include working with people from different religious or racial backgrounds. I have conducted workshops on storytelling and conflict resolution both at home and internationally.

I have also worked with political prisoners before their release under the terms of the Good Friday agreement which was part of the Northern Ireland Peace Process. This type of work remains as important as ever in the post-conflict situation and at a time when right-wing politics are on the rise and when a lot of racial prejudice is being seen in Europe and elsewhere including the United States.

Interviewers: Besides storytelling, what do you regularly do to advocate for peace or support efforts toward a more peaceful neighborhood/city/nation/world?

Liz: I believe this sort of effort must start within our communities, teaching our neighbors. I'm active in my own area, playing a part in community groups. Social media now affects millions of people, so I try to keep abreast of world news and share examples of international good practice.

Interviewers: Can you please describe some of the outcomes of your efforts to be a voice for or supporter of peaceful change?

Liz: Ninety-Five percent of schools in Northern Ireland are segregated according to religion. I regularly work with pupils from both sides of the divide and have seen the magic that happens when they get to know each other.

I wrote a series of television animations as part of the Media Initiative for Children, aiming to introduce preschool children to stories demonstrating anti-bullying, anti-racism, and anti-sectarianism.

Interviewers: Impressive! Who were your models or mentors for your work as a storyteller and/or voice for peace? What did they do that made them effective mentors or models?

Liz: I guess I was brought up in a family where tolerance and respect for others were highly valued. There have been role models in history promoting non-violence (Gandhi, Martin Luther King), but mostly my own experience of seeing needless killing shapes my views.

Interviewers: How do or how can the tools or gifts of storytelling support anyone's efforts to build a peace-filled community and create a peaceful world?

Liz: The act of listening to other people's stories shows respect for them, whether or not we agree with their opinions.

Interviewers: What actions would you want other people to take to make this world a more peaceful environment now, and for the generations to come?

Liz: Keep on telling stories and encouraging others to widen their horizons by traveling and meeting people whose backgrounds and experience are very different from their own.

Interviewers: Thanks so much, Liz, for making the time to share your experiences and insights. Peace!

NOTE

Liz didn't mention that she was the first winner of the International Story Bridge Award from the National Storytelling Network, USA, which cited her exemplary work promoting the art of storytelling.

Chapter Sixteen

Pick the City UP
#DROPTHEGUN #KEEPTHEPEACE
Susan Colangelo
President, Saint Louis Story Stitchers
Artists Collective

ONCE UPON A TIME, THERE WAS A STITCHER who liked to embroider stories from the newspaper. One day she was stitching about two sisters who were shot while sitting on their porch in University City, Missouri. One sister died. About a week later, two brothers were arrested for the crime.

The stitcher reflected on the power of stitching throughout history; of the AIDS Memorial Quilt and quilts used to signal safe passage to escaping slaves on the Underground Railroad. And she determined to join with others to create change. In August 2013, eight artists gathered in Old North St. Louis and founded the Saint Louis Story Stitchers Artists Collective—to make change.

The artists wrote the mission statement that night: to document St. Louis through art and word, to promote understanding, civic pride, intergenerational relationships and literacy.

Today, Saint Louis Story Stitchers Artists Collective is a 501(c)

(3) organization, where artists are in-residence on the beautiful stages of the Kranzberg Arts Foundation and in a Storefront Studio in the hip Loop District.

The Saint Louis Story Stitchers Artists Collective is professional artists and minority youth ages fifteen through twenty-four working together to create social change with a focus on gun violence prevention. Stitchers collect stories, reframe and retell them through art, writing, and performance to fulfill the organization's mission. Projects are platforms for community engagement through an artistic lens. The Saint Louis Story Stitchers shift perceptions and realities and bring hope to the Saint Louis community. Artists and the young create better understanding, justice and a healthier, more peaceful society. Art can save lives.

To understand Story Stitchers, think back over time through the field of artistic practice in social justice. Think of children's building blocks that form a growing tower. The words on the blocks include historic incidents which involve human tragedy, artistic movements, and social movements.

For example, in the history of the Civil Rights movement in the United States, there is a strong example of systemic change generated, in part, through storytelling. It is well recognized that Dr. King was a skilled orator and a mesmerizing storyteller. So, we had blocks that said Jim Crow Law, Segregation, Discrimination, Dr. King, Civil Unrest, Boycott, Vietnam, Military Draft, March, and Police Brutality. Added to the tower were blocks of art such as music ("We Shall Overcome," "Keep Your Eyes On The Prize," Bob Dylan's "Only A Pawn In Their Game"), works of photographers such as Gordon Parks and Bill Hudson, and videography of journalists showing dogs tearing at protesters' flesh, and the blasts of fire hoses. These shocking and undeniable images entered the living rooms of American families through the evening news. Our art helped to tell the stories, solidified change in American hearts and minds and helped to bring about justice. The resulting pressure generated a toppling of the status quo and the signing of the Voting Rights Act of 1965.

Another example is the AIDS Memorial Quilt. The quilt was conceived in 1985 by Cleve Jones, a gay activist working in San Francisco. In 1987, Cleve and his colleagues encouraged survivors to create quilts three by six feet describing their loved one, and send them to the project. Today there are more than 48,000 quilts commemorating people who have died from AIDS. The NAMES Project Foundation cares for and exhibits the quilt and has raised over $3 million for AIDS service organizations. The quilts—a massive community effort and outpouring of grief—helped Americans to visualize and understand the enormous number of lives lost to the AIDS epidemic. They helped put pressure on Congress to fund medical research and to create and enforce AIDS and illness-related anti-discrimination laws. The social consciousness of the country changed, one stitch, one tear, and one story at a time.

When people come together to work collectively for social justice they can create a strong impact. Artists can help to tell the stories that will move hearts and minds. These are lessons from history that Story Stitchers demonstrates. In this work, there is an inherent belief that art and word are essential ingredients to the creation of the social justice needed to create a peaceful society. There is also an understanding that the work must be grounded in the community it serves. For Story Stitchers, this is the African American community of St. Louis.

Story Stitchers artists-in-residence and youth come from economically disadvantaged neighborhoods in St. Louis city and county. Youth come through jobs programs, internships, friends, social media, open auditions, parents, or performances. The messages are raw and authentic. The stories are combined and rewritten, thus creating needed distance from the actual trauma the individual artists and youth have endured. When performers go public, it is collective stories they tell. Their own personal stories are woven within the fabric but not identifiable to any one person.

∞

Michael Brown was shot on August 9, 2014. The turmoil

surrounding his death boiled over into the streets of the city. Marches and protests blocked streets and disrupted cultural performances. Anger seethed and the national spotlight was unfamiliar, bright and burning.

By the fall of 2014, the teenage boys in Story Stitchers were fed up with the media about Ferguson. They asked who are these people all over the news? What do they know about what life was like for Michael Brown? They don't live here. Why don't they ask us? We know more than they do about this issue. They expressed frustration about exposure to bias, especially when out with a group of friends. From this discussion two pilot programs were created: the Youth Art and Writing Contest, Coming Of Age In St. Louis, which gathered stories from fifth to twelfth grade youth in the spring of 2015 and Perception Isn't Always Reality, which asked local artists to send in videos and photographs on the theme of implicit bias that the Collective would then loop together and publicly screen at Kranzberg Arts Center.

The entries received from both projects made it clear that gun violence was a pressing issue, especially for young African Americans. Feeding the violence was implicit bias. Examples follow:

Touch the Sky
Saivion, Grade Six

Don't try to put a ceiling on my sky;
Don't try to limit how high my dreams can fly,
Another 187 in my neighborhood ... everyday dreams
die,

I'm infusing my dreams with my own perception of
reality,
I'm struggling everyday to be all I can be,

In a world who wants to see the end of me.

Black lives matter? But the sidewalks are covered in

blood splatter.
Black blood spilled on concrete,
Black bodies look like me dead in the street.
Trying to please my momma and I don't want to be my father,
But the system is fighting against me,
I am 12 years old, will I be gunned down for having fun with a BB gun?
Found guilty before the trial people screaming, "Yes, he's the one"?

Young, gifted and black wearing a hoodie walking from a corner,
Eating skittles is subject to be killed,
Like a strange fruit hanging from a popular tree... a modern 2015 Emmitt Till.
Don't tell me my dreams aren't heaven sent!
You may have written the book but I'm the one selling it.
I'm Muslim so I ain't giving up dreams for Lent.

For every sound of a jail cell close,
For every tear from a mother that falls,
"Momma, watch me!" Your baby boy stands tall.

My dreams can only be limited by me!
Defined by me!
Followed through by me!
And realized by me!
Don't try to put a ceiling on my sky,
Try to limit how high my dreams can fly,
Another 187 in my neighborhood ... every day somebody's dreams die.

∞

Don't Shoot, Listen
Rachael, Grade Ten

How do I feel safe
when cars are more regulated than guns,
When mental illness is a stigma
instead of a treatable disease,
and when checking a background
before handing out a lethal weapon
Suddenly became an invasion of privacy?

Understand, I don't want to take your gun away
really; I don't want your gun.
I just want my blood to run coursing through my veins,
not onto the pavement.

I want my children to go to school
to learn how to create,
Not how to destroy.

And I want to stop feeling
like all the stripes on the American flag
should be red.

So please—don't shoot—just listen.

In May of 2015, the Collective added a storefront studio for recording, editing, and publishing in the hip Loop District, a favorite destination for music-loving youth. One hot summer Saturday morning K.P. Dennis came in and said that his nephew, Jacobi Taylor, had been shot and killed senselessly in the Jeff-Vander-Lou neighborhood. Gun violence came directly into the family of a leading artist in the Collective. As a result, there was a very palpable and determined turn to focus more clearly on gun violence as the number one issue affecting youth, artists, and our communities.

In the fall of 2015, the exhibition "Guns in the Hands of Artists" was to be shown at the Des Lee Gallery at Washington University in St. Louis. The exhibit consisted of art made from decommissioned guns by artists in New Orleans at the Jonathan Ferrara Gallery. Story Stitchers artists and youth wrote a proposal to create two new songs to perform at the artists' panel to bring local, authentic voices to the forefront. The proposal also included a youth-led discussion that explored what youth can do to help prevent gun violence. The proposals were funded by the Sam Fox School of Design and Visual Arts, the Institute for Public Health's Gun Violence Initiative at Washington University, and by the Regional Arts Commission.

To prepare, artists and youth met at the Storefront Studio to research gun violence in St. Louis. We wrote things of interest on the chalkboard wall. We found staggering statistics: In St. Louis in the past five years, 15,000 victims had been murdered, shot or robbed at gunpoint. The St. Louis Circuit Attorney reported there were 2,092 shootings in St. Louis in 2015 and half of them involved young people aged twenty-five or under.

We found a website by the St. Louis Circuit Attorney that said, "You need to know, you need to care, you need to act, the time is now." There was also a list on this site of the ten things we can all do to help combat gun violence. K.P. Dennis looked at the wall and wrote the beat and chorus to "Not Another One!"

> You need to know, you need to care, you need to act!
> Can't take it back!
> Not another one falling victim to the gun clap!!
> Not another one! Not another one!
> Not another one! Not another one!

He put the beat on the speaker, playing loudly, and the teens started writing their verses. This became the story song.

NOT ANOTHER ONE!
Stitchers Teen Council

You need to know, you need to care, you need to act!

Can't take it back!
Not another one falling victim to the gun clap!!
Not another one! Not another one!
Not another one! Not another one!

You need to know, you need to care, you need to act!
Can't take it back!
Not another one falling victim to the gun clap!!
Not another one! Not another one!
Not another one! Not another one!

You need to know, you need to care, you need to act!
Can't take it back!
Not another one falling victim to the gun clap!!
Not another one! Not another one!
Not another one! Not another one!

M-O M-O get the memo
When I say MO I say Missouri,
Listen close to my theory

Seem like MO problems MO sirens
Say MO sirens "MO sirens" Missouri silence,
Doesn't exist, ball up your fist, feeling the power
Open your hand, taking a stand, call' em a coward
For making a plan, illegal weapons
Don't be testing, watch yo head, when you stepping
That's just stressing
Keeping track of the death man
Too many eyes been squinting.
How you hate and don't even know, another victim.
One! I say no MO!

Never knew it could resort to this,
Pointless killing, no purposes.
A long track of dead corpses,

This world changed metamorphosis.
I don't want people to know the Lou,
As a place where people shoot,
Or a place where people loot,
Or a place where cops are brutes!

Show Me State let's show them then,
That disputes don't have to end!
With a life that has to end.
These streets, they can be cleansed
It starts with just me and you,
With this power, it can all be through.
This world sick it has the flu,
Let's make a change starting with the Lou.
Concentration leads to dedication, in order to
dedicate you need some patience.
Think about these situations; it could be another life
saving.
Living life where there always sirens,
Watch the news another man dying.
Face the facts and stand up!
Change the world and man up!

You need to know, you need to care, you need to act!
Can't take it back!
Not another one falling victim to the gun clap!!
Not another one! Not another one!
Not another one! Not another one!

You need to know, you need to care, you need to act!
Can't take it back!
Not another one falling victim to the gun clap!!
Not another one! Not another one!
Not another one! Not another one!

Not another one down
Not another one dead.
Playin with a gun yea it lead to the Feds,
You gotta put the gun the down leave it where it's
found.
Keep it unannounced gotta leave it out of bounds.
Gotta stop the violence stop it now
Not another one dead
Not another one down!
Pop one off now,
Addicted to the sound.
Pop pop pop now another down,
A call from the Feds now you lookin' at time.
Gave you a choice but you picked up the nine!
Now another one dead,
Not another one down.

We been there and we back again.
Killing people just to gain friends.
Drop da gun and pick up a book.
Can't read a sentence wanna play crook.

U a sad boy cause u ain't a man.
Ya life goals shot without a plan.
Thinking dumb cause u down to rob.
Ain't makin' money ain't gotta job.
U another one u can change that.
It's all different cause da pain's back.
U heard da boys and so u ran.
U another one and I'm not a fan.

© 2015, Saint Louis Story Stitchers Artists Collective

Next came the action song, "Gunshots!!" K.P. wrote
"Gunshots!!" with the third verse stating the Circuit Attorney's list

of ten things we can all do to combat gun violence in street rap.

Gunshots!!
K.P. Dennis

Every day is surviving... I'm a walking testimony!
Don't listen to that silly rapper cuz he's just a phony!
He rap about guns but he don't know that life!
A contradiction his reality don't coincide!
I know what's happening imagine me on they level!
Unfathomable... Too conscious so I can't settle!
Or wrap my head around it why people be so evil?
Carrying dirty guns concealing them is illegal!
But worst than that, you're turning' em on your own kind!
Killing each other, which brother gone end up in that pine?...
Wood box no socks and six feet!
The other gone get time... Jammed up with heat!
A baby girl died I cried can't bring her back!
These bullets ain't got no names!
God ain't blessing no trap!
These blasphemous buffoons adding fuel to the flames!
Bragging on their shooters all they do is bring us pain!
When we...

Hangout... gunshots!
Stay inside... gunshots!
Non stop... gunshots!
Daylight there's gunshots!
Nighttime more gunshots!
Around the clock... the young drop!
Wave your hands high if you're tired of hearing gunshots!

This is a movement; pretense to revolution.
The Renaissance is change so we can stop losing...
Somebody every day to senseless acts of violence!
Be on your merry way can't fix the problem with
silence!
People, let's talk about don't just be a bystander!
Need to develop a system that can provide answers,
To this contemporary crisis ain't speaking ISIS.
Domestic terrorism leaving neighborhoods lifeless!
Right in America, the war is in our backyard!
Travel for years and we still ain't made it that far!
To where we can say that it's ok and people civilized!
Does anybody care if the future lives or dies?
And I advise, to-the-wise... Better-listen to the young!
Before they mess up and do something dumb!
These guns... These lack of funds no resources!
Support this! It's no longer safe on front porches!
Can't...

You need to know, you need to care, you need to act!
Can't take it back!
Not another one falling victim to the gun clap!!
Not another one! Not another one!
Not another one! Not another one!

Secure ya legal weapon tell others to do the same!
Don't carry nothing if it ain't registered in your name!
Record the make, model, serial number information!
If it come up missing then you can find the location.
Call 911 whenever you hear some gunshots!
Tell the police if you witness a crime on your block!
If an organization improves the life of the youth,
Donate or volunteer your time and give 'em a boost!
Help a struggling parent... Whose burdens weigh a ton!

Become a mentor "earn and learn" hire the young!
They say I am the one! I guess I'm on the list,
Clean up my neighborhood participate in ownership!...
Make it a model gotta look out for each other,
If we get to know our neighbors we could fix it like
sisters and brothers!
I can't trust ya. How can we ever begin?
To build peace! I keep, losing my friends when they ...

You need to know, you need to care, you need to act!
Can't take it back!
Not another one falling victim to the gun clap!!
Not another one! Not another one!
Not another one! Not another one!

© 2015, K.P. Dennis/Saint Louis Story Stitchers Artists
Collective

Story Stitchers works in multi-year collaborative projects. Each
work builds upon past work. Members finish one another's sentences.

Story Stitchers released both songs on iTunes and produced
music videos for each song. The songs were used in the edited video
of the 2015 youth-led discussion on gun violence. Stitchers Teen
Council 2015–16 Co-Chairs Taron and Emeara, both seniors in high
school at the time, led the discussion. Youth invited police and civic
leaders to participate.

The discussion was transcribed and published as a book, *Not
Another One! A Discussion on Gun Violence,* available from Lulu. The
transcribed discussion was also utilized to create a script that was
commissioned by artist-in-residence Lauron Thompson. The script
was then staged by the Collective as a play at the .ZACK with Lauron
directing the production and K.P. Dennis directing the music. The
Collective has plans to work with three-time Emmy Award-winning storyteller Bobby Norfolk to develop a school assembly from
the script. Evaluation with teachers, counselors, and police will be

developed and coordinated by Sarah Hobson, Ph.D. of Community Allies, LLC.

A poem was commissioned from Stitchers youth leader Emeara for the play. Emeara took stories around her to create a story about growing up in a neighborhood affected by gun violence.

DIFFERENT
Emeara, Age 19

I remember those days when we'd be in the sun, but you'd have that gun. So I'd look into the
distance and tell you there's no need for that, we're just having fun.
But you'd say, "This is what it means to be a man. You wouldn't understand."
And I didn't.
I didn't understand how a piece of Iron could make you more of a man
than what you already were.
Then it came to me days later. You were searching for something.
Lurking over your own shoulder.
Trying to find answers from your past.
So you hide behind that mask. Thinking that your broken smile will get you by. Not for long.
I came along and tried to pick up the broken pieces that you had left behind.
Time after time I told you
to listen to your right mind.
But you still went left and left pieces.
Broken pieces.

You could never find the whole you, so only half of you lived while the other half died.
You grew cold and would lie about everything. Just to

deny the pain.

Trying to gain power.

It crippled me to see you grow sour.

I knew those guys who were supposed to be your boys would bring you down.

I told you.

I said I'd seen this site before.

September 11, 2001.

The only difference is that this time you were the building and your boys were flying the planes.

You made your life stand still just to let them burn it down.

And word around town is you're killing now.

Not like you're killing with the new J's, or even with puns and punch lines.

They're telling me guns and caution tape.

I'm still trying to remember what happened to you not joining gangs, but here you are again.

Behind another cell. Then you tell me, "I kilt him because he was trying to take my sells."

After that, I knew you'd never be the same.

You had some type of beast inside of you that couldn't be tamed.

So I decided to stay in my lane. I want no part in your games.

No Bonnie and Clyde.

No Ride or Die.

I just wanted the old you back, but we couldn't see eye to eye.

© 2016, Saint Louis Story Stitchers Artists Collective

During the summer and fall of 2017, the Collective took music and parts of this performance work into neighborhoods, community centers and cultural venues in economically disadvantaged African American communities for the Pick the City UP Tour. Pick the City UP Tour is about young people and gun violence prevention. #DROPTHEGUN #KEEPTHEPEACE

Lt. Col. Ronnie Robinson, Deputy Chief of Police, St. Louis Metropolitan Police told Story Stitchers, "Criminal activity amongst teenagers in the city is at a very high rate and unfortunately they do have access to illegal weapons. We need intervention and outreach along with enforcement in order to solve the ills that we are suffering from in our city relative to violent crime involving teens."

Pick the City UP promotes gun violence prevention through storytelling and innovative public health education. It is an intervention. The Tour helps youth understand that gun violence has many societal causes and the solution will require a multi-faceted approach that involves everyone working together.

Pick the City UP Tour is about learning ways to better love ourselves and one another. The Tour is about learning how to be safe, to feed our bodies and our minds so that we can be happier, healthier and wiser. It will give young people something positive to do, new music to enjoy, and will showcase peers who talk to police without fear, who advocate putting guns down, and who bring a new way of carrying oneself and of seeing one's future.

In order to see the systemic change that the Collective seeks, a broader audience will need to be reached. The dream is that the book will be utilized in university and high school classrooms, in police training and juvenile detention centers. The music will be incorporated into peer-to-peer public service announcements on television screens and radio stations across the country. The play will be performed by high school groups across the country. The youth-led discussion format will be picked up by a television station and incorporated into a regular broadcasting schedule. Hearts and minds will shift and see African American children and youth as they truly are — incredible young people full of promise.

NOTE

All poetry printed with deepest gratitude, with the permissions of Susan Colangelo and the St. Louis Story Stitchers.

Chapter Seventeen

The Holocaust, Littleton, & Our Children

Regina Ress

IN THE SPRING OF 1999, at the height of the Kosovo ethnic cleansing, I was invited to teach the Holocaust in the schools of Palm Beach County, Florida. (Florida is one of seven states that mandate Holocaust studies.) This was an amazing invitation, or as I saw it, "assignment." I created two different programs, one, a poetry process for classrooms and the other, a storytelling assembly.

In preparation, I searched for folktales and other stories that dealt with themes I might address. I read a lot of material on the Holocaust, talked with a survivor from the Warsaw Ghetto, and forced myself to look at photographs. On the plane to Florida, I read Yaffa Eliach's Hasidic Tales of the Holocaust.

I arrived in Florida two days before the shootings at Columbine High School in Littleton, Colorado. The day after the shootings was my first day in the schools. Between the ongoing images from Kosovo, my immersion in the Holocaust, and the news coming out of Littleton, my heart was torn open. I found myself crying suddenly, at odd moments. I was working principally in Middle schools and on wide open campuses. There were bomb threats at a couple of the local schools and feelings were running high, both of sadness and apprehension.

I questioned myself, "What are you doing in the schools at this moment?"

My answer was, "Doing something for the kids." I was wading into the situation; introducing a hard and painfully relevant topic; bringing information, metaphor, opportunity to question; offering a means of expression and a chance to be heard.

In my classes and assemblies, we looked at the need to stop hatred and violence before it gets out of control and affects the whole community (see "The Duel of the Cat and the Mouse," *Tales of Mogho,* Guirma); we looked at strength and power versus killing (see "Strength" in Margaret Read MacDonald's *Peace Tales*); we looked at megalomaniacal leaders (see H.C. Andersen's *The Wicked Prince*). As I led the students through the poetry process, we looked deeply at personal loss. I then shared with them the history of Terezin concentration camp and the art and poetry created by the children imprisoned there (see *I Never Saw Another Butterfly,* Volavkova). We talked about prejudice, inclusion, compassion. We talked about whatever the students brought up.

The students' responses were varied—as varied as the schools and grades I was working in. During my three-week residency, I taught in grades four through ten in private, public, and an alternative school for potential drop-out children of the sugarcane workers out by Lake Okeechobee. Many of the young people wanted to share things they knew about the Holocaust. Some asked really good questions. One seventh grade student asked about how much the United States knew and what did we did to stop the killing. "That's a very good question," I replied, but before I could find my way in and out of that enormous topic, another student brought up the incident of the St. Louis, the ship filled with refugees to which the United Stated refused entry. (It returned to Europe and most of its passengers perished.)

One of the poems about personal loss, written by a tenth grader, was about losing the "ground beneath my feet." What an incredible springboard from which to talk about what happened to the victims of the Nazis! The discussion in that class about losing everything in one's reality—physical, relational and even personal identity—was rich and deeply serious.

The stories, too, were marvelous springboards for discussion. With "The Duel of the Cat and the Mouse," the discussion led to the many excuses we make not to get involved, the "bystander" issue. The fact that we often equate bullying, hitting, and even killing with "power" and "strength' is shown starkly in MacDonald's story. After my telling of the Andersen story, there were discussions not only about Hitler, but other historical tyrants, the situation in Yugoslavia, and how sometimes young people follow the wrong leaders.

A number of the students brought up Kosovo. And sometimes the topic of the Littleton killings, which hung around the edges of our discussions always, found its way in to the center. In one "gifted" class, it surfaced after a rather lengthy discussion of Holocaust issues brought up in our story/poetry session. I left them with their teacher, hotly debating the role of the media in reporting school violence. They needed to talk about it, and our session had provided a forum.

To be in the schools, at that moment, was an enormous responsibility and a grand opportunity. Without talking directly about Littleton, a minor incident in the history of the world, but, at that moment, a major incident in the world of America's schoolchildren, we addressed some of the issues swirling around their reality. And I was there not simply with hard facts, endless statistics, and terrifying images, but with stories and poetry. I was there with images that touch the soul, spark the imagination and invite compassion.

The week after I returned to New York City, at a New York Storytelling Center Board meeting, we began talking about the Littleton, Colorado massacre. Mike Selliger's son had shown him something from the Internet about how young people feel we grownups would do as usual: agonize over the Littleton incident and then forget about it ... and them.

"Let me speak to that," I said. Having just returned from my experience in the Florida schools, I spoke about the opportunities we storytellers have to address, both indirectly and directly, the serious concerns with which our children are wrestling. Indeed, we storytellers are a blessed group. Through image and metaphor, through the seemingly simple vehicle of story, we have the chance to address the BIG themes of the human soul. As always, I am grateful to be working with story.

Notes & References

This article is reprinted with the generous permission of Regina Ress. It was first published in the December 1999 issue of *Storytelling Magazine*.

Anderson, H.C. *The Wicked Prince.* College Station, TX: Creative Company, 1840, 1995.

Eliach, Y. *Hasidic Tales of the Holocaust.* New York: Vintage, 1998.

Guirma, F. "The Duel of the Cat and the Mouse." *Tales of Mogho: Stories of Upper Volta.* New York: Collier Macmillan, Ltd., 1974.

MacDonald, M.R. "Strength." *Peace Tales: World Folktales to Talk About.* Hamden, CT: Linnet Books, 1992.

Volavkova, H. *I Never Saw Another Butterfly: Children's Drawings and Poems from the Terezin Concentration Camp, 1942-1944.* New York: Shocken, 1994.

Chapter Eighteen
Barry Stewart Mann: An Interview
Sherry Norfolk and Lyn Ford

Interviewers: Hi, Barry. Thank you for your willingness to share a bit of yourself in this small effort to approach a big issue. For those who may not know you and your work, please tell us who you are, where you live, and how long you have been a storyteller.

Barry: My name is Barry Stewart Mann. I live in Atlanta, Georgia. I've been telling stories professionally since about 1991.

Interviewers: What types of stories do you share?

Barry: I share all kinds of stories. I share stories in programs in schools and libraries, so I offer folktales, literary tales, personal stories, historical stories, biographical stories, and original stories. Sometimes they are organized in thematic programs, such as trickster tales, or stories about the winter holidays, or stories from American History, or stories about scientific inventions. In the programs I develop for libraries, I always connect with literature, and often do retellings of stories from popular books.

Interviewers: Where do you do most of your storytelling or other work?

Barry: My storytelling is primarily at schools and libraries, with other venues including camps, festivals, community events, private celebrations, and more. In other work, I lead storytelling and drama workshops with children in schools and with teachers in professional development settings; for this part of my life, I work with a theatre, several arts organizations, and a number of universities. Geographically, most of my work is in the Atlanta metro area, or around the state of Georgia. Over the past couple of years, through my connections with universities, I have also worked in Florida, the Carolinas, and in several states in the western US. I am delighted at the prospect of a storytelling tour I'll be doing in Colombia.

Interviewers: Has your work changed over the years? If it has, when and why did you begin changing or doing your work?

Barry: Hard to say. I began as an actor, so the addition of storytelling was a big shift, and over the past decade, I have done less and less acting and more and more teaching. In both teaching and telling, there has been a subtle shift to connect more directly with curricular topics—STEM/STEAM, Science, Social Studies. I have programs such as "Who Put the Fizz in My Pop?" and "Chavez and Johnson", and workshops including "Science and Drama—Really?" and "Storytelling and Math."

Interviewers: What does the word "peace" mean to you? What is your vision of a peaceful world?

Barry: It starts with inner peace, which moves outward to the ability to accept and adapt to changing circumstances, and by extension, the ability to accept and honor others. That acceptance and respect is the basis for peace between individuals, and from there, peace among groups, clans, communities, states, and nations.

Interviewers: Beautiful statement. Was there any experience in your life that pushed you to become an advocate for peace? In just a few sentences, can you share that experience?

Barry: I would have to say the defining experience might be the move my family made when I was twelve years old, relocating from a fairly monocultural, middle-class community in suburban New Jersey, to a very diverse city in southern Florida. It happened at my transition into junior high school—a jarring enough transition to begin with, but, in my situation, I found myself swimming in a sea of accents, lifestyles, and demographies. I think that opened my eyes in a way they likely would not have been opened in my bedroom community up north.

Interviewers: Those experiences at a young age surely influenced who you are now. Do you consider yourself a deliberate advocate for peace, or do you consider your storytelling an organic experience for building community?

Barry: I have been known to march in the march, or to pick up a protest sign, but in the main, I think my work for peace follows the wisdom of the bumper sticker that reads, "If you want peace, work for justice," and my work for justice involves encouraging all, especially the "you", to become aware of and develop empathy for the "Other"—the stranger, the oppressed, the underdog, the illiterate, the less-abled, the more flawed in any story, be it a folktale about a noodlehead like Juan Bobo or the Sages of Chelm, a devised drama about bullying, or an imagined scene of the first contact between Columbus' crew and the Taino on Guanahani (an island in the Bahamas). I think these approaches encourage students and listeners to hear the missing voices in a text or story and to imagine the multiple sides of an issue. It really is about empathy, just empathy through imagination. Which, I suppose, describes all empathy, because we cannot really know another's feelings, but only imagine.

Interviewers: When and why did you begin to feel you were a "voice for peace"—an advocate or supporter of some effort toward bringing effective communication, comfort, social justice, or useful change into the world?

Barry: I believe it has been a process over the years, as I have worked more and more, at first by chance and then by choice, with disempowered populations, such as those at public high schools who face challenges I cannot imagine, or those at the elementary school where I've been doing after-school programs for nearly a decade, believing that the best I can offer them, even more than the puppetry and the folklore, is the consistency of my showing up.

Interviewers: Those young people truly benefit from your consistently being there for them. Are you deliberately active in other efforts toward peace at a local or regional or national or international level?

Barry: I would not say that I am active in this capacity. I have been involved politically: canvassing, phone banking, engaging in voter registration, driving people to the polls. I have attended various marches and demonstrations over the years. At this point in my life, a small bit of activism comes in the form of supporting my teenage son, who has achieved a certain level of fame on social media as a spoken word artist addressing issues of justice.

Interviewers: It's so important to support the voices of our young spoken-word artists, and of anyone who is willing to speak out for social justice. Besides your own spoken word art of storytelling, what do you regularly do to advocate for peace or support efforts toward a more peaceful neighborhood/city/nation/world?

Barry: I try to live my life in a way that engenders peace through example and simple actions. I have for most of my adult life lived in a co-housing community, a form of intentional community that uses consensus for decision making, strives to live sustainably, and engages in community activism. I try to live in a manner that is environmentally responsible, driving a hybrid car and having solar panels on my home. While not identical with the impulse toward peace, I believe that environmental responsibility is more closely connected to peace than we tend to think. Many conflicts in the world (Syria, South Sudan) have arisen out of the management, and scarcity, of resources like food and water.

Interviewers: Yes, responsibility at home impacts responsibility in the larger world community. Were there any models or mentors for your work as a storyteller and/or voice for peace? If there were, what did they do that made them effective mentors or models?

Barry: My storytelling mentor was David Novak—internationally renowned storyteller, and a National Storytelling Network Circle of Excellence Oracle Award recipient—and what made him an effective model as a voice for peace was his capacity to weigh multiple viewpoints, and to see the complexity, nuance, and deeper meaning in even the simplest of stories.

Interviewers: How do or how can the tools or gifts of storytelling support anyone's efforts to build a peace-filled community and create a peaceful world?

Barry: Storytelling invites story-listening, and good storytelling helps people discover, or rediscover—as it is something we all had as small children—their capacity to listen at length, with an appreciation for detail, and with empathy.

Interviewers: What actions would you want other people to take to make this world a more peaceful environment now, and for the generations to come?

Barry: I would want people to listen more, and opine less; to weigh their words; and to avoid taking things personally, or thinking that every story they encounter requires a direct and personal response, judgment, or evaluation.

Interviewers: Thanks so much, Barry, for making the time to share with us. Peace!

NOTE

What Barry didn't say is that he is a graduate of Harvard University with an M.F.A. in Theatre from the University of San Diego, and was a featured teller at the second Festival Internacional de Cuentacuentos in Santo Domingo, Dominican Republic.

Chapter Nineteen

The Strength of Butterflies
Lyn Ford

"We delight in the beauty of the butterfly, but rarely admit the changes it has gone through to achieve that beauty."
—Maya Angelou

SOME CALL HER SISTER RUTH. I CALL HER MIZ RUTH. Others know her as the wife of the late Dr. Hugh Morgan Hill, better known as the poet and storytelling advocate, Brother Blue.

She is Ruth Edmonds Hill, scholar, educator, oral historian, and advisor for national and international organizations that promote and perpetuate the spoken word. Miz Ruth is also a part of the Radcliffe Institute for Advanced Study at Harvard University, where her oral history office is located. The content of her heart has brought her recognition that is not limited by the color of her skin. And she is as beautiful and as strong as—a butterfly.

Her efforts to preserve the voices of women, in collections of interviews now known as the *Black Women Oral History Project: From the Arthur and Elizabeth Schlesinger Library on the History of American Women,* [at that time part of] Radcliffe College by Ruth Edmonds Hill (1991), and the *Illustrated Women of Courage:*

An Exhibition of Photographs, which became the book of the same title, by Judith Sedwick and Ruth Edmonds Hill (*Radcliffe College: Arthur and Elizabeth Schlesinger Library on the History of Women in America: Black Women Oral History Project,* 1984), aren't as well known as the support she gave to her husband and partner in life, Brother Blue.

Her success in preserving the homestead of Reverend Samuel Harrison is a story rarely heard or known beyond its Massachusetts setting. Rev. Harrison, who was born in 1818 and who became pastor of the Second Congregational Church in Pittsfield, Massachusetts, and of Sanford Street Congregational Church (now St. John's Congregational Church) in Springfield, Massachusetts, was chaplain of the first all-black regiment to fight in the Civil War, the 54th Massachusetts Volunteer Infantry. The 54th is better known than Rev. Harrison or his great-granddaughter, Miz Ruth, thanks to the dramatization of its exploits and harrowing experiences in the movie, *Glory.*

The 19th-century Samuel Harrison House still stands at 82 Third Street in the Morningside neighborhood. It is now a museum, thanks to the efforts of Miz Ruth, Brother Blue, and the Samuel Harrison Society.

Miz Ruth doesn't brag about any of it. You have to listen to her as she is interviewed, and witness the strength of a butterfly. The butterfly is a symbol of importance for both Miz Ruth and Brother Blue, who died in 2009.

Butterflies don't make noise. At times, they silently rest. But when they fly, they are a burst of color that "speaks" not just to the eye, but to the soul.

Brother Blue, the more outgoing of the two activists, often said of Miz Ruth, "I'm just a fool. I am learning from her."

Painted on the palms of his hands were blue butterflies. His signature motif was the metamorphosis of a caterpillar into a butterfly and the hopes and dreams through which that change was made.

At the time of his death, Brother Blue had been a soldier (honorably discharged after serving as First Lieutenant in the segregated US Army in World War II), a student (receiving a BA cum laude in Social Relations from Harvard College in 1948, accepted into the Harvard Graduate School of Arts and Sciences, before transferring to the Yale School of Drama to receive a MFA, and a Ph.D. recipient (Divinity with pastoral sacred storytelling) from the Union Institute), a street performer in Harvard Square, an actor in a George Romero film (Brother Blue played Merlin in the 1981 movie, *Knightriders*), and Official Storyteller of Boston and of Cambridge. Like the blue Morpho butterfly that was his totem, Brother Blue and Sister Ruth were admired, welcomed and loved around the world.

"Brother Blue frequently exhorted people to tell 'stories that change the world,' with the combination caveat-encouragement, 'We want a story from your heart. If it's not from your heart, don't tell it.'" So said Henry Louis Gates, Jr., presenting the 2009 W. E. B. Du Bois Medal from the W. E. B. Du Bois Institute at Harvard University to Ruth Edmonds Hill for Brother Blue.

Writer and social worker Kristen D'Angelo says, "Peace dwells on wings of butterflies." The fluttering of their wings can be considered a call to action and change for the beauty and betterment of the world. That is the story that butterflies perpetuate.

Story—"… bread for the mind, the imagination, the heart, the soul."—Dr. Hugh Morgan Hill, better known as Brother Blue, on storytelling. Quoted at http://www.artofstorytellingshow. com/2007/10/07/brother-blue-on-street-storytelling/

Mr. Hill regarded storytelling as a sacred duty and a path to universal harmony. "When you tell a story, you tell it to all creation," he once said. "It's cosmic. It never goes away." http://www.nytimes. com/2009/11/27/arts/27hillobit.html

Notes & References

In 2003, Yellow Moon Press published *Ahhh! A Tribute to Brother Blue and Ruth Edmonds Hill*. Edited by Robert Smith, it is still available in paperback on Amazon.com.

Northeast Storytelling (NEST) named an annual award for its original recipients in 2002, Brother Blue (a.k.a. Dr. Hugh Morgan Hill) and Ruth Hill. The award honored them for their unfailing promotion of storytelling and storytellers throughout the region of New England. Brother Blue said the award was intended "to honor those who give their lives to storytelling to change the world."

Information for this article was gathered both from personal experiences and from "Wake Up and Smell the Poetry" video, April 2015, at https://www.youtube.com/watch?v=EyI-moXiloE

https://en.wikipedia.org/wiki/Ruth_Edmonds_Hill

https://www.nestorytelling.org/brother-blue-and-ruth-hill-award/

http://archive.boston.com/ae/theater_arts/articles/2009/11/09/cambridge_storyteller_brother_blue_remembered_for_compassion_inspiration/

http://www.nytimes.com/2009/11/27/arts/27hillobit.html

Part Three
Wonder

WONDER

"Curiosity, amazement, marvel, caused by the beauty of the unknown or inexplicable, and combining into a strong desire to know, or know more."
—Lyn Ford

Sitting at the feet or on the lap of an elder, wrapped up in a blanket of love and stories, enchanted by the beauty of language and ideas that transported us to places that never really existed... Climbing the cherry tree in our backyard, ready to travel a universe of creative thought born on the wings of the pages of books ... discovering solutions to or release from troubles because I had a mind filled with possibilities ... these were the gifts of storytelling that I received as a child, the gifts I tried to pass on to my own children, and, now, to their children.

Here are stories for your journey in possibilities for peace. Stories shared can lift those possibilities from hope and thought to growth and promise.

Please know that all the stories in this chapter are the storytelling authors' adaptations of old tales. They are offered for you to see their promise and adapt it to your own voice, your style of telling. Sit at the feet of their tellers, wrap yourself in their love, know their beauty and enchantment, and share as a gift of change for the world. As you make that journey of wonder, know that you are not alone. The message of peace is still being carried on the voices of storytellers.

Chapter Twenty

A Portrait of Peace
Adapted by Regina Ress
From a story by Linda Spitzer

"The more clearly we can focus our attention
on the wonders and realities of the universe about us,
the less taste we shall have for destruction."
—Rachel Carson

THERE WAS ONCE A KING WHO WONDERED what peace looked like. As he was a wise king, he called upon the artists of the kingdom to help him. He announced that he would give a prize to the artist who could create the best portrait of peace.

Many artists brought pictures. Some of the pictures were big and some were small. Some had many colors, some were in black and white. The king looked at all of them. He looked and eliminated and looked and finally … there were two paintings left. But only one could win the prize. He had to choose one of them.

The first painting was of a beautiful, calm lake surrounded by green mountains. The lake was so calm, it was like a mirror … showing the mountains, the blue sky and the fluffy white clouds floating peacefully above it. Oh, yes, everyone agreed that this was a perfect picture of peace.

The second one also had a lake. And it also had mountains. But these mountains were rocky and bare. The lake reflected a gray sky with dark clouds. Lightning flashed and rain was falling. There was a tumbling waterfall on the side of the mountain. How could this be a portrait of peace?

But the king was a wise king and he looked closely at what the artist had painted. Behind the waterfall was a small tree clinging to the rocks. In the arms of the tree was a nest and on the nest sat a mother bird. There, in the middle of that storm, the mother bird sat on her eggs. She was a perfect picture of peace.

The king chose the second picture. He understood that although peace can be found in a place where there is no trouble, no noise, no anger, it can also be found in the midst of things as they are, when there is calm in your heart.

"That," he said, "is the true meaning of peace."

Notes & References

Linda Spitzer's story was included in the book, *Stories to Nourish the Hearts of Our Children in A Time of Crisis*, edited by Laura Simms. (www.laurasimms.com)

The story was also posted in 2001 at http://healingstory.org/portrait-of-peace/ by Linda Spitzer.

Linda's story, titled "Portrait of Peace," was also used as the introduction to the book, *Peaceful Places: Boston: 125 Tranquil Sites in the City and Beyond* by Lynn Schweikart. Menasha Ridge Press, 2013.

For more information about Linda Spitzer's work, go to http://storyqueen.weebly.com/

Chapter Twenty-One

The Animals' Peace Treaty
A fable from Chad,
Retold by Lyn Ford

"You'll never find a rainbow if you're looking down."
—Charlie Chaplin

THE FIGHTING AND QUARRELS BETWEEN ANIMALS of one kind or another had taken a great toll on every creature's life and kin. After much discussion, the surviving animals decided that, in order for them to continue to exist, a peace treaty must be created and signed. Once this was done, all the animals would live together like one big, contented family. And if there were to be any battles, they would be carried out as a united front against the enemy of all, the two-legged creatures called *Humans*. Humans were animals that sometimes killed for sport instead of for the necessities of food, warm skins, and bones for making their tools. Human men, women, and children sometimes mistreated creatures who did not walk, communicate, and live as they did. The animals decided they would be better than these "human" things, and would treat one another with more than tolerance; the animals would treat all beings with loving kindness and deep respect.

Messengers were sent out to announce the wonderful news of the new peace treaty. They traveled to every corner of the world and called out to every creature, "Peace! There will be peace! A peace treaty is being signed by the elders, and a party will be held to celebrate this historic event! There will be no more wars, unless we must battle against the cruelties of the two-legged ones!"

The next morning, animals joyfully gathered at the appointed place, an enormous field beside a beautiful river, where there would be room for everyone who could attend. Big creatures stood carefully beside small ones; carnivores and omnivores suppressed their appetites so that vegetarian creatures could safely stand with them; birds sat upon the backs of snakes; fish leaped from the waters, not to eat the insects who congregated, but so that they might hear at least a little of what was said.

And much was said! Notable representatives from various species made long and elaborate speeches about the peace treaty. All rejoiced when the speeches were over; whether their rejoicing was for the speeches, or for the fact that they were over is still a matter of discussion among the birds and the beasts.

Then it was time for dancing, to the music of the songbirds, accompanied by the chattering of monkeys, and the drumbeats of the elephants' stomping feet.

But some grew tired. It is not easy to be pleasant to others when one is too tired. And some grew intolerant—the eagles wondered why they should have to share the same tree with lesser fowls, and the rhinoceros shook his horn at the thought of lightly stepping around ugly critters like turtles and frogs.

And some became hungry. First their stomachs growled, then their sneering mouths. Their hunger justified their vision—other creatures appeared to be potentially tasty meals, rather than potential friends. Soon, hyena sat and drooled on a stammering nanny goat. The eldest queen of the lion's harem stealthily led her entourage toward the zebras. A panther leaped upon a giraffe's back.

The ensuing confusion and panic caused terror among the

smallest creatures, who screeched and squealed warnings to anyone who might hear. And the most powerful among the strongest fought amongst themselves about who would now be in charge.

The two-leggeds heard the commotion in the field. They came with guns, knives, arrows, spears—and fear. The field became quiet. The only ones who remained there were the dying and the dead.

The peace treaty was never created or signed. Thoughts of the peace treaty did not even last until sunset. But the animals no longer spoke to one another of war against the humankind. There was no need, for the two-leggeds fought many wars amongst themselves. Their peace treaties are often broken.

And the memories of hunger, anger, fighting, and fear remain among all to this day.

In Chad, a moral is shared for this story:

Peace and harmony do not come from speaking clever words;
above all are behaviors and actions.

Note

This moral and its story are adapted from one in *Paroles d'hier et d'aujourd'hui : Ainsi parlaient nos ancêtres*, Djimtola Nelli. CEFOD-Éditions, BP 87, Sarh, Chad, 1995.

Chapter Twenty-Two

Mountain Lion and Human
A Folktale from Chile
Adapted by Milbre Burch

ONE MORNING, HIGH IN THE MOUNTAINS OF CHILE, Mountain Lion asked her mother, "Hey, Mom, is there anyone braver, stronger, and smarter than mountain lions?"

She expected her mother to say no, but instead, the old one shook her head and said, "There is one who is braver and stronger and smarter than mountain lions. He is called Human, and though he is little, he is clever and that makes him dangerous. It is because of him that we live so high in the mountains, because he very rarely comes here.

Mountain Lion could not believe her ears! "There cannot be anyone braver and stronger and smarter than mountain lions! I'm going to find this Human and I'm going to fight this Human! And then we'll see what's what!"

Her mother could do nothing to dissuade her, so she gave her blessing to her child. That day Mountain Lion left the mountains that had always been her home.

She traveled down, down, down, till she came to a field. And there she saw a Horse. Mountain Lion had never seen a horse before. She said: "Are you Human? Because if you are, I've come to fight you! Then we'll see if you are braver and stronger and smarter than mountain lions! Are you Human?"

"Neighhhh," said the Horse, "But Human is my master. And if he wants to get someplace in a hurry, he jumps upon my back and rides me. If I don't go fast enough, he kicks my sides with spurs! See how I am wounded on either side!"

"He treats you like that and yet you stay here?" asked Mountain Lion.

"Yeahehehehehess," said the Horse.

"Then you're a slave to the Human!" said Mountain Lion.

"Yeahehehehehess, Human is my master!"

"Well, I'm going to find this Human and I'm going to fight this Human and then we'll see what's what," replied the Mountain Lion.

So she kept traveling, down, down, down till she came to a second field. And in that field, there was an Ox. Mountain Lion had never seen an ox before. She said: "Are you Human? Because if you are, I've come to fight you! Then we'll see if you are braver and stronger and smarter than mountain lions! Are you Human?"

But the Ox shook his head and said: "Mmmmooo, no! But Human is my master. And if he has a heavy load to carry, he puts a yoke around my neck and I must pull and pull and pull his load in a wagon. My shoulders get very tired."

"He treats you like that and yet you stay here?" asked Mountain Lion.

"Mmmmooo, yes!" said the Ox.

"Then you're a slave to the Human!"

"Mmmmooo, yes!" said the Ox, "Human is my master!"

"Well, I'm going to find this Master and I'm going to fight this Master and then we'll see what's what," replied the Mountain Lion.

So she kept traveling down, down, down till she came to the

foot of the mountain that had always been her home. And there in a field she saw a Dog, blinking in the sun. Mountain Lion had never seen a dog before. She said: "Are you Human? Because if you are, I've come to fight you! Then we'll see if you are braver and stronger and smarter than mountain lions! Are you Human?"

"No!" barked the Dog, "But Human is my master. He tells me what to do and I do it! And I love him very much!"

"He tells you what to do and yet you love him?" asked Mountain Lion.

"Yes! We are the best of friends!" barked the Dog.

"Then, you go tell your friend that Mountain Lion is here to fight him!"

The Dog leapt up and ran to the house where he lived with the Human and barked, "Master! Mountain Lion is in your field and wants to fight you! Bring your gun and come with me!"

Human took his gun and followed the Dog to the field where Mountain Lion awaited him. When she saw this two-legged creature with hardly any fur at all, she could not believe her eyes. "You're Human??? I can't believe that you are braver and stronger and smarter than mountain lions! I've come to fight you!"

Human said, "I have no quarrel with you. If you want to fight, we must call each other names, say mean words, make each other angry. Then we can fight. You go first."

Mountain Lion said, "I think you are a cruel Master and a slave-driver who forces others to work for him. And all the animals hate you, except that stupid Dog right there!" And then she stuck her tongue out at Human and said, "Nyah!"

Human said, "All right, you have hurt my feelings with your mean words. And I only have one word to say to you!" With that, Human lifted his gun, and as he fired, he shouted, "Bang!"

"Ouch!" cried Mountain Lion. With a stinging shoulder, she ran past the Human and the Dog, up the mountain past the Ox, up the mountain past the Horse. She did not stop running until she reached the top of the mountains that had always been her home.

And there she licked and licked and licked her wound.

She told her mother: "I found Human and called him every bad name I could think of and didn't hurt him at all. He said only one bad word to me—Bang!—and it burns like fire! If he had said many words to me, my skin would be in tatters! I hope I never see Human again!"

And because Mountain Lion lived the rest of her life high in the mountains of Chile, she never did see Human again.

Notes

I first read this Chilean folktale in a print collection titled *The King of the Mountains: A Treasury of Latin American Folk Stories* edited by M.A. Jagendorf and R.S. Boggs (New York: Vanguard Press, 1960). In that volume, the story is called "Lion and Man." It was early in my storytelling career and I was eager to represent female characters who were neither blonde nor sleepy. Thus, I changed the Mountain Lion from "he" to "she."

Even though the boastful behavior of the main character may "read" as archetypally masculine behavior, females are often expected to lean in and adopt behavior that is used to get ahead in male-oriented workplaces. Please note that rambunctious female characters populate imaginary workplaces in folk tales (like Norway's "Tatterhood") and tall tales (like *America's Sally Ann Thunder Ann Whirlwind Crockett*) across the continents.

Meanwhile, animal research tells us that it's the females among big cats who are most likely to be the hunters in a pride. Chile's Patagonian Pumas are raised by their mothers in forests and on steppes or rocky slopes in the mountains before becoming mostly solitary adults.

I have told this tale to primary age children in elementary schools for years, asking them afterward to consider whether Human would have defeated Mountain Lion if he hadn't brought his gun—an unknown object to his adversary—to the match. I included the story on my (now out-of-print) audio cassette, *Treasure on the Tongue* (Columbia, MO: Kind Crone Productions, 1999).

"Strength," a Limba tale from West Africa in *Peace Tales: World Folktales to Talk About,* edited by Margaret Read MacDonald (Little Rock,

AR: August House, 1992), is a similar story, calling out the assumed superiority (and trickery) of humans when dealing with their relatives in the Animal Kingdom. For years I have told that tale to upper elementary students and included it on my (now out-of-print) audio cassette, *The World is the Storyteller's Village* (Columbia, MO: Kind Crone Productions, 2001).

Sherry Norfolk pointed out the motif of assumed human superiority over animals—even animal royalty—in Aesop's fable, "Lion and Man." She also pointed out to me a story called "Brother Lion and Brother Man" retold by Tyrone Wilkerson in *African-American Folktales* edited by Richard and Judy Dockery Young (Little Rock, AR: August House, 2006). Wilkerson's tale is clearly a fraternal twin to my Chilean adaptation. His even puts into words what the above tale leaves unsaid: "If Mister Lion didn't know what Man was, he sure didn't know what a shotgun was" (p 64).

Copyright, Milbre Burch, 2017. Printed with and grateful for the author's permission.

Chapter Twenty-Three

The Legend of Sleeping Lady
A modern-day folk legend
Retold by Sherry Norfolk

"It has been said that without imagination there is no forgiveness, no love, no moving out towards each other—surely qualities so desperately needed in these troubled times."
—Series editors' preface, p. xii, *Supporting Creativity and Imagination in the Early Years,* by Bernadette Duffy

COOK INLET STRETCHES 180 MILES from the Gulf of Alaska to Anchorage in south-central Alaska. The inlet is surrounded by snow-capped mountains, one of which is called the Sleeping Lady.

The Lady hasn't always slept there. Long, long ago, before the inlet was explored and settled by Dena'ina people, before Russian fur hunters came, before Captain Cook sailed up its shining waters, a tribe of giant people lived along those shores.

In that long-ago time, the people lived in peace. There was no reason for hatred or war or fear.

In one of the villages, the people were happily preparing for the wedding of a young man named Nekatla to a young woman named

Susitna. Everyone knew that the two were deeply in love, and they were excited to see them wed.

But a few days before the ceremonies, they noticed acrid smoke on the northern horizon. Men set out to learn what was happening to their neighbors, and to help if needed. On their way, they met a stranger, exhausted and wounded. They hurried to his aid.

"What's happened? How can we help you?"

"My village has been attacked," he gasped. "Warriors from the north destroyed our village, killed our people, and burned our homes! My family is dead... I only escaped because I was out on the sea when it happened, and arrived too late to help my people. But I have to help others—I have to warn others that these people are cruel and bloodthirsty!"

All plans for the wedding were forgotten. Instead, the people began to plan for survival.

War was not their way. They didn't have weapons, nor did they know how to fight. Hiding in the forest might save lives, but their homes would be destroyed.

Nekatla and Susitna listened in silence.

Finally, Nekatla rose.

"There is another option," he began. "We cannot fight these people and neither can we hide or run away. But perhaps we can teach them a better way, which is peace."

People began to nod their heads, their eyes beginning to alight with hope.

"Explain your idea," the elders encouraged him.

Nekatla continued, "This is my proposal: instead of running, we go north to meet them. We will carry gifts rather than weapons so they'll have no reason to attack us. We'll convince them to lay down their weapons and live in peace. I am willing to go first."

It was a terrifying plan, but it made sense to the people, who had lived all their lives in peace. Soon it was agreed: all the men of the village would go. Everyone began preparing for the dangerous journey, packing up the treasures that were to have been wedding gifts for the happy couple, the food that was to have been served at the celebration, chanting for peace.

Soon, the men were ready to leave. Sadly, Susitna and Nekatla stood on a hill above the village, saying farewell.

"We will be married as soon as this is over," promised Nekatla.

"I will wait for you right here, where we last embraced," answered Susitna.

The men set off in silence, leaving their loved ones with heavy hearts.

Susitna watched until they were out of sight, then prepared to wait. She gathered her needles, knife, and baskets, then climbed back to the top of the hill and busied herself gathering nuts and berries.

When she had gathered all the nuts and berries that were ripe, she began cutting roots and grasses to weave into baskets. Then she began to weave. After many hours, her baskets were finished, but the men had not returned.

Her fear and worry growing, Susitna tried to keep busy. She sewed. She wove. She gathered. She watched. Her eyes were red with exhaustion, but she could not, would not, sleep. She could only gaze north, watching for the first sign that the men were returning, that Nekatla was safe.

The days turned into weeks. Susitna still could not sleep for worry and dread, but at long last, she was too tired to sit up. She stretched out on the hillside…and finally, she slept.

She was still sleeping when word of a terrible battle reached her village.

"Nekatla was very brave," reported the young boy who had escaped. "He led our men to meet with the warriors. But before he and their leader could speak, someone threw a spear and killed him! That started a battle—their men attacked ours and we fought as best we could with no weapons. We fought until all our men were dead or dying, and many of theirs, too."

He named the men—fathers, sons and brothers—who had been lost to the village as the women and children wept.

Susitna slept on.

Finally, the women agreed that they must wake her and tell her the horrible news. They climbed up the hillside and found her, sleeping peacefully in a bed of wildflowers.

"Let her rest," said one, and they all nodded sadly. Why break her heart any sooner than necessary? They wove a blanket of soft grasses and wildflower blossoms, which they gently laid over her, then went quietly away, leaving her to dream of Nekatla.

Back in the village, all joy and warmth had fled. The air grew colder and colder, and Susitna slept on. All around her, the women of the village continued to weep, their tears turning to flakes of snow. One teardrop, one flake at a time, snow began to cover the land. It also covered the sleeping form of Susitna, still stretched across the hillside.

Thousands of years have passed since that long-ago time. But Susitna still sleeps on her hillside, dreaming of Nekatla's safe return—dreaming of peace.

The people say that when peace rules the earth, then Susitna, the Sleeping Lady, will awake.

Let us hope that she awakens soon.

Notes

Alaska myths are rural legends

Mount Susitna, known as Sleeping Lady, has long been a jewel in Anchorage's panoramic crown of mountains across Cook Inlet. The historical tale describes the mountain as resembling the profile of a woman asleep, long hair stretched out behind her. Everyone knows the story comes from Alaska Native lore, right?

Wrong, according to Nancy Lesh, a University of Alaska Anchorage librarian. Lesh wrote a story about Sleeping Lady in the early 1960s as a senior in high school, and published it in *Alaska Northern Lights* magazine. "I think I made the story up, although I can't definitely say for sure," she said.

Ann Dixon, who published the children's picture book *The Sleeping Lady* in 1964, agreed that the story is not a Native legend. Instead, Dixon said, the tale probably originated with prospectors or homesteaders sometime between 1930 and 1950. In Dixon's version, the giant woman fell asleep waiting for her beloved to return from battle, unaware that he had been killed.

In the 1980s, a woman who had written a postcard with a Sleeping Lady story sued a songwriter for copyright infringement, Lesh said. Dixon and her publisher also were sued for their version of the story, but a judge ruled that the story had become a legend, and was therefore uncopyrightable.

In *A Dena'ina Legacy,* Peter Kalifornsky told the story of the mountain people who gathered at Susitna, and a giant lady who said she would lie down by the river she loved to become Susitna Mountain. Her relatives followed, Kalifornsky said, to become Mount Redoubt, Mount Iliamna and the Chigmit Mountain Range. Another wandered inland to become Denali.

Cook Inlet Region Inc. Historian A.J. McLanahan has cited evidence that Mount Susitna was sacred to the Dena'ina people in the area, and linked the mountain, which they called *Dghelishla,* or *little mountain,* with Denali, which they called *Dghelay Ka'a,* or *big mountain.* McClanahan stated in the *Anchorage Chronicle,* "These stories are better than the made up legends, They really deserve more credit than they get."

Chapter Twenty-Four

Holding Up the Sky
A Chinese Fable
Adapted by Lyn Ford

"The more I wonder, the more I love."
—Alice Walker, The Color Purple

AN ELEPHANT SAW A HUMMINGBIRD. The tiny creature wasn't flut-tering and darting about, as a hummingbird is wont to do. This hummingbird rested, motionless and silent on its back, and held its minuscule feet toward the sky.

Of course, the elephant became very curious. She asked, "Little, little, little bird, what on earth are you trying to do?"

The hummingbird quickly replied, "Oh, didn't you hear? Word is spreading that the sky might fall today. I don't know if that's true, but I have made myself ready to help if such a thing truly happens. If the sky falls, I am here, ready to hold it up with my feet."

The elephant laughed until her huge trunk snorted and she could hardly breathe. When she could finally speak again without chuckling, she taunted the hummingbird: "Little, little, little bird! Do you, so small that you can scarcely be seen, really believe that your small and insignificant feet could possibly hold up any portion of the magnificent sky?"

The hummingbird thought for just a second, then grinned. He kept his legs pointed toward the sky, and his feet up in the air. He answered, "Well, no, I couldn't possibly hold up any portion of the sky all by myself. No, not alone. But when something is wrong, each of us must do what we can as best we can, for the sake of all of us. And, being willing and being ready, this is what I can do."

NOTES & REFERENCES

Nobel Peace Prize Laureate Wangari Maathai, founder of the Green Belt Movement in Kenya, tells the story of the hummingbird attempting to put out a forest fire by picking up droplets of water from a stream again and again and again. Other animals hopelessly watched the fire and chastised the hummingbird for his efforts. But the hummingbird continued, and stated, "I am doing what I can."

Chang, I. C. *Tales from Old China*. New York: Random House, 1969.

MacDonald, M.R. *Peace Tales: World Folktales to Talk About*. Hamden, CT: Linnet Books, 1992.

MacDonald, M.R. *Three Minute Tales: Stories from Around the World to Tell or Read when Time is Short*. Little Rock, AR: August House, 2005, p.145.

Chapter Twenty-Five

Gratitude for a Gift
A Hindi teaching tale
Adapted by Lyn Ford

"For most of human history, 'literature,' both fiction and
poetry, has been narrated, not written—heard, not read.
So fairy tales, folktales, stories from the oral tradition, are
all of them the most vital connection we have with the
imaginations of the ordinary men and women whose labor
created our world."
—Angela Carter

AN OLD STORY SPEAKS OF A YOUNG MAN who was crossing a desert
to get to the village of an elder man who would be his teacher. The
air was hot and dry and the sun beat down on the young man, but he
saw something in the distance. It was grass, and a few bushes, all fed
by a spring of clean, clear water. The young man drank, then filled
his leather canteen with the water. He thought this sweet, cool water
would be a wonderful gift for his teacher.

The journey to the elder's village took more than a day. Some
say it took four days to reach the school. But the young man smiled
as he entered a beautiful garden, where an old man sat and talked

to many students. The young man bowed to his teacher; he told the story of his long, difficult walk, then gave his canteen to the old man. "I wanted you to have some of the sweet water I found," he said. "I wanted to thank you for giving me an opportunity to learn."

All the students in the garden watched as the elder took a long, slow drink of that water. He smacked his lips and smiled. "Ahhhh," he said to the young man, "Thank you for such a wonderful gift!" The young man, tired and thirsty and hungry, smiled a big, satisfied smile and went into the elder's house. This would be the young man's school and home. He thought of how grateful he was for his chance to get an education. He thanked the elder's servants for giving him a little food to eat, plenty of water to drink, and a bed where he could take a long rest.

Another student asked the teacher if he could also taste the water that seemed to give so much satisfaction to both the giver and the recipient of the gift. The teacher again smiled, and handed the leather canteen to this student. The student took a long, slow drink form the canteen. Then he spat water everywhere, and shouted, "This is awful! The water is warm, and rank! It smells and tastes like leather! Teacher, why did you thank that boy for this horrible water? Why did you say it was a wonderful gift?!?"

The elder sighed, "Child, you have so much to learn. You tasted only the water. I tasted that young man's gift. He walked for more than a day to get here. He could have used that water, I'm sure. But he gave it to me.

"The leather canteen held more than water. It also held an act of loving kindness and gratitude. There is no sweeter gift than that."

Note

This story has been shared as both an Arabic story and a Hindi moral story on various websites.

Chapter Twenty-Six

Tears on the Moon's Face
A Kabyle Folktale from Algeria
Adapted by Lyn Ford

LONG AGO, THERE WAS AN ORPHAN CHILD who wandered the earth alone. He had no father; he had no mother, he had no village, he had no one. Whatever had happened to his people was of no importance to the rest of the world. Nobody seemed to care for him or to wonder why he was so sad. But, despite his sadness and solitude, the boy did not weep, for the universe was still so new that tears had not yet entered the world.

The child did not weep, but oh, how he wailed! His voice carried beyond the horizon, and all the way up to the moon. Hearing this voice, so full of pain and anguish, people covered their ears. But the moon looked down upon the orphan boy and felt deep compassion. The moon left his place in the sky, and stood before the boy. Then he reached out to the child and rested upon the ground with the child gently cradled against his chest.

"Weep," said the moon, "let your pain fall like rain. But we must not let your tears touch the earth; we cannot let such sorrow in salty tears drop to the earth, for they would make it unclean for planting.

"Dear child, let your tears fall on me. I will carry them back to the sky, and you will know some relief."

The orphan child pressed his face against the cheek of the moon. The boy slowly breathed in, and felt the first tears ever to fall. His tears rolled down his cheeks and dropped upon the face of the moon. And the moon spoke a blessing as he comforted the boy: "From this moment on, if one such as you should weep, every person shall love you."

The people who had covered their ears could not muffle the sound of the weeping orphan child. Their hard hearts softened. They found themselves searching for the one who cried. Exhausted, but somehow hopeful, the child shed his last tear. The moon returned to the sky. And the people came, and immediately loved the boy. They took him to their village; they tended to his needs. They gave him love. He was an orphan no more.

To this day, when you look at the moon's face, full and bright in the night sky, you will see the stains left by the tears of a weeping child. They are the first tears ever shed in the world.

Notes & References

http://www.algeria.com/folklore/

This story was also adapted by Amy Friedman and Meredith Johnson for their column, "Tell Me a Story," which is syndicated with Andrews McMeel Syndication and appears in newspapers and at the website uexpress (http://www.uexpress.com/tell-me-a-story/2002/7/28/tears-on-the-moon-a-north). The story as it is printed there makes both the moon and the weeping child female characterizations. Although it is noted as "A North African Tale," its source is not cited.

Also, see:

Jablow, A. & Withers, C. *The Man in the Moon: Sky Tales from Many Lands.* "The First Tears" (p. 10). New York: Holt, Rinehart & Winston, 1969.

Chapter Twenty-Seven

The Bear and the Bees
A Northern Italian Fable
Adapted by Lyn Ford

ONCE, A HUNGRY BEAR DISCOVERED A FALLEN HOLLOW TREE in which he could smell the aroma of his favorite treat. A swarm of bees had stored their honey in the fallen tree's trunk. Some of them were resting in their hive, and some of them were busy gathering nectar in a field of clover.

The bear sniffed and snuffed at the honey, ready to take what he wanted. A single worker bee came back from the field of clover, and saw the huge and hungry bear. To protect her home, she bravely flew at the bear and stung him, zap!, on his nose. Then she disappeared into the hollow trunk, and waited, ready to protect her home and family.

That bear raged in anger and yowled in pain. With sharp claws and teeth, the bear tried to destroy both the tree and the beehive inside it. But this only awakened all the bees in the hive, and brought all the workers back from their nectar gathering. The whole swarm surrounded the bear, stinging him everywhere, yes, everywhere.

Now sore from the tips of his ears down to his toes, the bear dove into a pond to save himself. He had no honey, and no inclination to get it. He was still hungry, but he was wise enough to admit that he had tried to steal the honey and destroy the bees' home. The bear knew that he would have been better off if he'd walked away from a single sting than he was flying into a rage and feeling a hundred more.

Note

"De urso et apibus," from Laurentius Abstemius' Hecatomythium (1495). The fable has long been attributed to the fables of Aesop, but, in fact, is rooted in stories from Northern Italy that were incorporated into the Aesop compilation associated with Martinus Dorpius (alias Maarten van Dorp, 1485–1525).

Chapter Twenty-Eight

The Virtuous Wife
A Moroccan folktale
Retold by Sherry Norfolk

RASHID KISSED HIS BELOVED WIFE AMINAH goodbye as he prepared to set off on his pilgrimage to Mecca.

"I hate to leave you alone, my love, but I have asked my brother to watch over you and keep you safe until my return. Be well, and know that I will come back to you."

Aminah wiped the tears from her eyes and tried to smile.

"Allah be with you."

"And with you."

Aminah watched until Rashid was out of sight, then turned back into her tiny home. Everything was worn and ragged, but clean and neat. She smiled to herself. "All will be well."

In his own palatial home, Rashid's brother, Harb, was thinking the same thing: "All will be well." He finally had the chance to pursue Aminah! He had always been jealous of Rashid's happy marriage and desirous of his faithful and loving wife. Immediately upon Rashid's departure, Harb began his campaign to steal Aminah's affection.

"I will shower her with luxuries that Rashid can never provide. She'll soon see how much happier she could be as my wife!"

He sent baskets of fine foods. She was grateful.

He sent beautiful flowers. She was confused—flowers were not the sort of gift a man should give to a sister-in-law. What was Harb thinking?

He sent silken scarves and jeweled rings. She sent them back. They were not appropriate or welcome gifts.

He knocked on her door. Aminah hesitated, but when she finally opened the door a bit, he pushed his way inside.

"Why have you sent back my gifts, Aminah?" Harb demanded. "I only want to make you happy!"

"You know that I cannot accept such gifts, Harb. These are the sort of things a suitor would send to his beloved. I am your brother's wife. You must leave me alone."

He grabbed for her arm, but she spun away. She reached the door and pushed it open. "Leave at once, Harb!" He scowled, but turned to go, then turned back.

"I always get what I want, Aminah, you should know that. And if I can't have what I want, then no one else will." He stormed away, and immediately began a defamation campaign against Aminah, spreading rumors that she was unfaithful to her husband.

At first, no one believed what they were hearing. Aminah was known to be virtuous; the rumors were dismissed. Harb came up with another plan. He began hiring men to knock on Aminah's door, asking for water or directions. As the townspeople saw man after man entering her modest home, their trust began to erode.

Then, Harb went on the attack. He gathered everyone in the center of the village and loudly proclaimed that his sister-in-law had been unfaithful to his brother. "She must be punished!" he declared. "Stone her!"

The townspeople took up the chant: "Stone her! Stone her!" and then took up stones and began to throw. They harried her to the edge of the village until she collapsed. There, they left her for dead, piling some of the stones on and around her.

She lay under the heavy stones for hours, slowly regaining consciousness. Injured and exhausted, she couldn't move, but when she heard camels and men passing by, she began to moan.

"What's this?" The men found the bruised and bleeding woman and decided to take her to the next village for help. They found a kind older couple who took Aminah in, nursed her wounds, and invited her to live with them.

As time passed, Aminah realized that Allah had given her the power to heal others. First the children next door, then an older neighbor – her fame began to grow outside her own village, reaching across the land.

Meanwhile, Rashid returned from his pilgrimage to the heart-breaking news that his wife had been stoned to death for infidelity. "Impossible!" he moaned, "She was the most faithful and loving wife in the world. I'll never believe these lies."

There was additional bad news: his brother Harb was gravely ill, and nothing that anyone could do had helped him.

"I can't save Aminah, but perhaps I can save you, dear brother," Rashid said. "In my travels, I have heard of a woman who is said to be a great healer. We will go to her immediately." Harb's great wealth made it easy to arrange a small caravan to allow the invalid to travel in comfort. They sent word ahead to the healer, asking for her attention.

When Aminah learned that her husband and brother-in-law were on the way to her, she prepared for their arrival by hanging a curtain behind which she could talk with the men without being seen. She practiced disguising her voice so that it would not be recognized.

"Tell me of your sickness," she said.

Harb related his symptoms and the efforts that had been made to heal him.

"Please help him," begged Rashid.

Aminah answered softly but firmly. "Your illness is not caused by a physical malady. You are sick because you have committed a dreadful wrong. In order to be healed, this sin must be confessed."

The sick man shook his head feebly. "I have done nothing

wrong. I am sick! Heal me!"

Aminah simply repeated," In order to be healed, this sin must be confessed."

A long silence ensued, followed by a spate of harsh coughing, and then Harb began to sob.

He whispered, "Rashid, I am ashamed and filled with remorse. Your wife is dead because of me. I told the village people that she committed adultery and encouraged them to stone her to death. My sin is indeed grievous, and I deserve to die. Please find it in your heart to forgive me, and I will spend the rest of my life atoning for the wrongs that I have caused."

As Rashid stared at his brother in dismay and disbelief, Aminah stepped around the curtain. Rashid's horror turned to joy, and the two embraced for a long, long time. Finally, Aminah looked deeply into her husband's eyes.

"I can heal Harb if you wish." Rashid looked at his weeping brother, and placed a compassionate hand on his shoulder.

"I love my brother, though he did a horrid thing. His confession and contrition are genuine. And you, my dear Aminah, are still alive. I forgive him, and beg you to cure him if you can."

Aminah complied immediately. The two brothers embraced, and Harb promised to confess his lies to the village upon their return. The villagers were overjoyed to receive Aminah back into the community, and the reunited couple lived in peace and harmony for the rest of their days.

Notes

Only forgiveness can allow all parties to move towards true peace. As Sharon Creeden comments in *Fair is Fair: World Folktales of Justice* (Little Rock, AR: August House, 1994), "Justice is not ultimately found in the legal system, but in the human heart."

This story is told variously as a Moroccan Jewish tale, a Greek folktale, and a Muslim story.

AFTERWORD

"Human salvation lies in the hands of the
creatively maladjusted."
—Dr. Martin Luther King, Jr. speech
Western Michigan University, December 18th, 1963.

BECOMING A FUNCTIONING ADULT OR EVEN YOUNG ADULT in society
is often summed up in the phrase, "being well-adjusted." And adjust
we must: to school policies, organizational rules, and civil laws. Yet
each of us has memories of encountering policies, rules, and even
laws that seem wrong, inappropriate, or outdated. In those circumstances, we have felt compelled to some degree to object. Sometimes
it is a matter of simple procedure or of moving into what feels like
a modern consciousness, but occasionally the urge to object comes
from a deeper place, a feeling that some cherished principle of
morality calls upon us to take a stand.

Sometimes, we feel the need to defend a concept so central
to our idea of a decent home, institution, or society that we cannot
compromise. To borrow Dr. King's phrase, "there are some things
concerning which we must always be maladjusted" if we are going
to be able to look ourselves in the mirror with respect. In Twentieth
and Twenty-first Century America, we have struggled with racial,
financial, and gender-based inequities that have limited the rights,
safety, livelihoods, hopes and dreams of generations. We must not
accept this as the status quo.

In the opening up of our government, business, and academia
to the diversity of minorities, women, and the LGBTQ community,
we have expressed our faith in people despite so-called differences,

and we have expressed our hope that justice will prevail over bias and discrimination.

∞

Creative ideas do not come from following the norm, sticking to the script, or repeating the past. Nor can a single individual do everything that's needed to change our world. But a single good word or deed can become an epiphany for someone. A single idea can become a shared thought process. A shared thought process can become a movement toward a new reality. The abstract can become concrete, through actions. And actions are needed every day.

While this book was being written, acts of violence and social injustice continued, not only in the United States, but around the world. For more information, go to https://www.hrw.org/world-report/2017/country-chapters/united-states, or simply view recent news reports on any night of the week. What you discover there will be tragic, perhaps overwhelming, but it is only part of the story, a story that loving hearts hope to end.

As Sherry and I put the finishing touches on this book, the peace was once again challenged. In August 2017, North Korean leader Kim Jong-un announced a plan to fire four test missiles that would land near the U.S. island territory of Guam. This plan included details such as the missiles' exact travel times and splash-down points. North Korea's announcement said that the waters of Guam would experience "an enveloping fire."

This rhetoric was said to be a response to President Donald Trump's August eighth statement that threatened "fire and fury" against North Korea if it did anything to endanger the United States. (*New York Times* articles, "Trump Threatens 'Fire and Fury' Against North Korea if It Endangers U.S.," August 8, 2017, by Peter Baker and Choe Sang-Hun; "North Korea Says It Might Fire Missiles Into Waters Near Guam," August 9, 2017, by Choe Sang-Hun; "North Korean Threat to Guam Tests Credibility of Kim and Trump," August 10, 2017, by Choe Sang-Hun)

On August 15, 2017, *CBS News This Morning* broadcast that

"North Korean state radio on Tuesday announced that President Kim Jung Un planned to hold off launching missiles at Guam, while the United States said it was ready to defend the territory." (http://www.cbsnews.com/news/north-korean-leader-kim-jong-un-holds-off-on-guam-missile-plan/)

But this was only one of the peace-shattering situations in the world. On Saturday, August 12, 2018, violence erupted in Charlottesville, Virginia, as white supremacists gathered for a Unite the Right march. Members of the Neo-Nazis, KKK, and other groups were challenged by counter-demonstrators. A cacophony of voices and viciousness that included mace and guns, makeshift weaponry and urine-filled balloons was met by police force. In the violence that ensued, a young man, James Alex Fields, Jr., drove his car into a crowd of peaceful counter-protesters who were walking to the nearby pedestrian mall. Nineteen people were injured, and a young woman, Heather D. Heyer, was killed. (https://www.nytimes.com/2017/08/13/us/charlottesville-protests-unite-the-right.html)

In all, at least thirty people were injured. In addition, two Virginia State Patrol troopers, Lt. H. Jay Cullen and Trooper Berke M.M. Bates, who were monitoring Charlottesville events from their helicopter, died when the copter crashed in a wooded area.

Threats of war, lost lives, broken hearts, unhealed wounds from ongoing struggles that began before the Civil Rights Era and calls for equal rights for all—this was the week of August 6 through 12, 2017. And a fire was lit, it was an enlightening, a flame in the hearts of empathetic people, something with the power to heal. "People around the nation marched Sunday [August 13] in support of [peace and change in] Charlottesville. There were more than 130 rallies from Maine to California, according to a CNN tally of events posted to social media." (http://www.cnn.com/2017/08/13/us/charlottesville-white-nationalist-rally-car-crash/index.html)

Among those rallying against extremist and racist violence were about 500 people in Goodale Park, Columbus, Ohio, my hometown. And a group of prayer warriors around the world began a new vigil of prayer, not just for Charlottesville, or Guam and North Korea, but for love and peace for every member of the world family.

Gaining more and diverse information is an essential stepping-stone for creating the path to change and a new promise of peace. Some articles from other websites worth visiting are:

https://religionnews.com/2018/11/13/fbis-new-hate-crime-report-captures-an-america-changed-by-hate/
https://hateinamerica.news21.com/
https://www.splcenter.org/hate-map
https://www.tolerance.org/

We have given you thoughts, words, deeds, and stories. Think about them, share them, talk about them with others, put the ideas into action. Doing will make the difference.

What will you do to nurture and uphold our rights to speak peace?

—Lyn Ford

ACKNOWLEDGEMENTS and CONTRIBUTORS

Milbre Burch, Ph.D.—a performer, playwright, poet, dramaturge, recording artist, archivist, activist and educator—is a storyteller in every sense of the word. A teaching artist since 1978, she received an NSN Oracle Award in 1999 and a Grammy nomination in 2007. She has appeared at the National Storytelling Festival eight times and told or taught at festivals, camps and conferences in Spain, Austria, Slovenia, Taiwan and the United Kingdom. *The New York Times* has praised her "classic wit," the *San Diego Union-Tribune* has called her "mesmerizing, like a fine solo dancer." With Berkley Hudson, she created the archival Storytelling Project of the Cotsen Children's Library at Princeton University. She has an article on Fairy Tale Performance co-written with Patricia Sawin in a book, *Routledge Companion to Fairy-Tale Cultures and Media* (2017).

Susan Colangelo, MFA, LSU '83, is the founding president of the Saint Louis Story Stitchers Stitchers Artists Collective. Susan brings 30+ years of community arts experience and work with six school districts as an artist and consultant to the organization. Specializing in large scale community-school-university programs, she developed WOW! World of Wonder for West Virginia University, bringing the arts to 20,000 school children, and coordinated the first contemporary African music and dance concert at the University of Georgia. Susan is an advocate of literacy and a proponent of reading aloud to the young.

Linda Schuyler Ford grew up in New York's Hudson Valley, listening to the stories of her Dutch-German ancestors and roaming the very hills that enchanted a young Washington Irving. A lover of folktales, her passion for therapeutic storytelling has been shaped by her work with health care professionals, caregivers and elders.

She also performed during a Healing Arts event for children in Newtown, CT. She now divides her time between Florida and New England. Contact Lynda StoriesHeal@gnsil.com www.SchuylerFord. com

Linda Goss (Mama Linda), was born in the foothills of the Smoky Mountains, Alcoa, Tennessee, and was a social activist in the 60s at Howard University and in Philadelphia. She is a published poet and author, and the co-founder, along with the late and beloved master storyteller, Mother Mary Carter Smith, of the National Association of Black Storytellers. Contact Mama Linda at nabsfounder@ gmail.com

Bob Kanegis, storyteller and story coach, lives by Vine DeLoria's admonition, "to be related somehow to everyone you meet." For more than twenty-five years he has led a life immersed in story-teaching, telling and coaching. Bob believes that everyone has two big stories to tell: The Story of Me and The Story of We, and by exploring those stories can build a strong foundation for themselves and a good relationship with each other and the earth. As a founder of Tales & Trails Storytelling, Bob has traveled the country, as a performer, workshop leader and Ambassador to the Realm of Possibilities. In his role as Story Coach, Bob focuses on the importance of telling stories skillfully and intentionally; finding right story, for right people, at right time. His reflections on storytelling have been anthologized in publications including *Where the Heart Is, The Healing Heart* (Families) *Tell the World* (Storytelling Across Language Barriers), and in articles in *Storytelling Magazine.* He is a past president of Storytellers of New Mexico and NM state liaison to the National Storytelling Association. Contact Bob at bob@storyconnection.com

Doug Lipman has traveled the world performing, coaching, and training others to tell, to teach others, and to make their livings doing what they love. He has taught storytelling skills to educators, healthcare workers, corporate executives, and death-penalty defense lawyers. You can subscribe to Doug's free e-mail newsletter (over 150 issues at this writing) at http://StorytellingNewsletters.com.

Barry Stewart Mann is a storyteller, actor, and arts educator based in Atlanta. He earned his B.A. from Harvard and his M.F.A. from the University of San Diego and the Old Globe Theatre. He is on the teaching and performing rosters of the Alliance Theatre, the Georgia Council of the Arts, the Teaching Museum, and ArtsNow, and teaches storytelling and drama integration in Lesley University's M.Ed. program in Integrated Teaching through the Arts. Barry has presented on drama and storytelling at the University of Florida, Utah State, Boise State, Georgia State, Emory University, and William Paterson University, He was named National Storyteller of the Year, was heard as a regular contributor to the public radio program "Recess!", and was a featured teller at the second Festival Internacional de Cuentacuentos in Santo Domingo, DR. Learn more at barrystewartmann.com and barrystewartmann@hotmail.com

Caryn Miriam-Goldberg is the 2009–13 Kansas Poet Laureate, and the author or editor of over twenty books, including most recently, *Miriam's Well*, a novel; *Everyday Magic*, non-fiction; and *Following the Curve*, poetry. She is founder of Transformative Language Arts at Goddard College, where she teaches, and she leads writing workshops widely on transformation through the power of our words. Goddard Graduate Institute. http://www.carynmirriamgoldberg.com, https://www.goddard.edu/academics/goddard-graduate-institute/

Bobby Norfolk is an internationally known story performer, teaching artist, three-time Emmy Award winner, multiple Parents' Choice Gold and Silver Award winner, Storytelling Oracle Award recipient, and author of *Eye to the Sky*, a memoir. Bobby is one of the most popular and dynamic story-educators in America today. Learn more at www.bobbynorfolk.com

Celine O'Malley received her Bilingual Multiple Subject and Single Subject in English teaching credentials from California State University, Chico, and works as a storyteller and teaching artist in Northern California. She highly recommends the resource, *Rethinking Multicultural Education: Teaching for Racial and Cultural*

Justice 2nd Edition by Wayne Au. (Rethinking Schools, 2014). Contact Celine at celine.omalley@gmail.com.

Regina Ress, award winning storyteller, actor, author and educator, has performed and taught in a wide variety of settings for over forty years from Broadway to Brazil in English and Spanish, from grade schools to Senior Centers, from homeless shelters and prisons to Lincoln Center and The White House. She teaches storytelling at New York University's Program in Educational Theatre and Program in Multilingual/Multicultural Studies. She has taught ESL/Public Speaking for Santa Fe University of Art and Design and is co-producer and board member of *Healing Voices-Personal Stories,* a documentary film company focused on domestic violence. Her CD *New York and Me: We're in a Long Term Relationship* won a 2014 Storytelling World Honor Award. Get in touch with Regina: storytellerrress@aol.com

Kenneth Roth is Executive Director of Human Rights Watch, operating in more than ninety countries and one of the world's leading international human rights organizations. See and download a PDF easy-to-read version of the World Report 2017 at https://www.hrw.org/sites/default/files/supporting_resources/hrw_world_report_etr_final_0.pdf

Kiran Singh Sirah is President of the International Storytelling Center (ISC), an educational and cultural institution dedicated to enriching the lives of people around the world through storytelling. ISC organizes the world's premiere storytelling event, the National Storytelling Festival, and supports applied storytelling initiatives across a wide variety of industries. Prior to his appointment at ISC, Kiran developed a number of award-winning peace-building programs in cultural centers across the UK. As an artist, folklorist, teacher, and advocate for social justice, he has used the power of human creativity to establish dialogue. An advisory member to UNESCO and a Rotary World Peace fellow, he has developed educational programs and publications, articles, talks and conference papers about interdisciplinary approaches to relationship building in communities and around the globe. Contact @storyconnect or http://www.storytellingcenter.net/

Jessica Senehi is Associate Professor in the Peace and Conflict Studies Program, which is within the University of Manitoba's Faculty of Graduate Studies and housed within the Arthur V. Mauro Centre for Peace and Justice at St. Paul's College. She is the founding director of the Winnipeg International Storytelling Festival: Storytelling on the Path to Peace / Festival international du conte de Winnipeg: Se raconteur une nouvelle histoire de paix. She is co-editor of Storytelling, Self, Society: An Interdisciplinary Journal of Storytelling Studies. Get in touch with Jessica: Jessica.Senehi@ umanitoba.ca

Jane Stenson, a retired educator, recently moved from Evanston, Illinois, to a small farm near Mineral Point, Wisconsin. Gardens where producing an environmental film festival is her focus these days, with weekly storytelling in the local school, state parks, and church. In 2016, Jane was honored to receive the National Storytelling Network's Distinguished National Service award based on her five books on storytelling, her leadership of NSN's special interest group Youth, Educators, and Storytellers Alliance (YES!). Always interested in integrating storytelling and education, Jane—with the help of the YES! Board—encouraged this group to produce a study of storytelling and the Common Core standards which can be found free of charge on the YES website. Contact Jane at http://janestenson. com or stenson.stories@gmail.com

Kristin Wardetzky includes among her many experiences: 1970–1991 theater pedagogue at the Central Theater for Children and Youth in East Berlin and from 1970–2007, professor at the University of the Arts Berlin. Her research focus is artistic narrative in theory and practice, children and youth theater, and fairy tale research. Kristin is the initiator of the course of studies, Storytelling in Art and Education, at the University of the Arts in Berlin, and chairman of the Verein Erzählkunst e.V. Kristin's awards include the Bundesverdienstkreuz am Bande, European Fairytale Prize. kristin.

wardetzky@gmx.de

Liz Weir is a storyteller and writer from Northern Ireland. She was the first to earn the International Story Bridge Award from the National Storytelling Network, USA, which cited her exemplary work promoting the art of storytelling. Liz has told her stories to people of all ages on five continents. As Children's Librarian for the City of Belfast during the Northern Irish Troubles she learned about the healing power of storytelling. In today's post-conflict era she still works with stories to promote cultural understanding and leads workshops on storytelling and conflict resolution both at home and abroad. www.lizweir.net

EDITORS

Lynette (Lyn) Ford is a mother, grandmother, great-auntie, and great-grandmother, who is also known as an award-winning storyteller and author, teaching artist, certified laughter yoga teacher, giver of hugs, and partner-for-life to the very patient Bruce Ford. Lyn feels honored to have shared stories and writing exercises with and encouraged spoken and written narratives from students in special needs programs, elders in adult care facilities, soldiers working their way through trauma, and story-sharers of all ages. Lyn's most recent publications are *Boo-Tickle Tales: Not So Scary Stories for Ages 4–9* (Parkhurst Brothers, 2017), and *Storytelling Strategies for Reaching and Teaching Children with Special Needs* (Libraries Unlimited, 2017), both written and edited with friend and fellow storyteller/teaching artist, Sherry Norfolk. More about Lyn may be found at www.storytellerlynford.com

Sherry Norfolk is an award-winning storyteller, author and teaching artist, performing and leading residencies and professional development workshops nationally and internationally. As a performing artist, she is a dynamic storyteller, telling well-crafted and age-appropriate folktales from around the world. As a teaching artist, she uses storytelling as a strategy for teaching preK–12 curriculum. She is co-author with dear friend Lyn Ford of *Storytelling*

Strategies for Reaching and Teaching Children with Special Needs (Libraries Unlimited, 2017) and *Boo-Tickle Tales: Not So Scary Stories for Ages 4–9* (Parkhurst Brothers, 2017); and with fellow storyteller and teaching artist Jane Stenson of *The Storytelling Classroom* series (four books that explore rigorous, standards-based storytelling strategies for learning across the curriculum). Sherry is a trainer for the CETA program at The Kennedy Center for the Performing Arts, Adjunct Professor at Lesley University, and a recognized leader in integrating learning through storytelling. www.sherrynorfolk.com

ADDITIONAL RESOURCES AND INITIATIVES
Sherry Norfolk

WISDOM & WORK

Print Resources for Peace & Social Justice

Abdel-Fattah, R. *Where the Streets Had a Name.* New York: Scholastic Press, 2010.

Alexie, S. *The Absolutely True Diary of a Part-Time Indian.* New York: Little Brown, 2007.

Alsenas, L. *Gay America: Struggle for Equality.* New York: Amulet, 2008.

Amnesty International. *Free? Stories about Human Rights.* Somerville, MA: Candlewick Press, 2010.

Aukerman, M. "'Why Do You Say Yes to Pedro, but No to Me?' Toward a Critical Literacy of Dialogic Engagement." *Theory into Practice.* Vol.51:42–48, 2012.

Bausum, A. *Denied, Detained, Deported: Stories from the Dark Side of American Immigration.* Washington, D.C.: National Geographic Children's Books, 2009.

Birtha, B. *Grandmama's Pride.* Park Ridge, IL: Albert Whitman, 2005.

Carmi, D. *Samir and Yonatan.* Translated by Yael Lotan. New York: Arthur A. Levine Books, 2000.

Castellucci, C. & Rugg, J. *The Plain Janes.* New York: Minx, 2007.

Coman, C. *Many Stones.* Honesdale, PA: Front Street, 2000.

Compestine, Y. C. *Revolution Is Not a Dinner Party.* New York: Henry Holt, 2007.

Cooper, P. *When Stories Come to School: Telling, Writing and Performing Stories in the Early Education Classroom.* New York: Teachers and Writers Collaborative, 1993.

Cox, A.M. & Albert, D.H. *The Healing Heart for Communities: Storytelling for Strong and Healthy Communities.* Gabriola Island, BC Canada: New Society Publishers, 2009.

Cox, A.M. & Albert, D.H. *The Healing Heart for Families: Storytelling to Encourage Caring and Healthy Families*. Gabriola Island, BC Canada: New Society Publishers, 2009.

Creech, S. *The Unfinished Angel*. New York: Joanna Cotler Books/HarperCollins, 2009.

Crowe, C. *Getting Away with Murder: The True Story of the Emmett Till Case*. New York: Phyllis Fogelman Books / Penguin, 2003.

DeSaix, D. D. & Ruelle, K.G. *Hidden on the Mountain: Stories of Children Sheltered from the Nazis in Le Chambon*. New York: Holiday House, 2007.

Durrell, A. & Sachs, M. (eds.) *The Big Book of Peace*. New York: Dutton, 1990.

Ellis, D. *Three Wishes: Palestinian and Israeli Children Speak*. Madeira Park, BC, Canada: Groundwood / Douglas & McIntyre, 2004.

Exley, R. & Exley, H. *My World Peace: Thoughts and Illustrations from the Children of all Nations*. Lincolnwood, Ill.: Passport Books, 1985.

Flake, S. *Money Hungry*. New York: Jump at the Sun/Hyperion, 2001.

Fox, J. *Poetic Medicine: The Healing Art of Poem-Making*. New York: Putnam, 1997.

Fredericks, L. *Using Stories to Prevent Violence and Promote Cooperation*. Boulder, CO: Colorado School Mediation Project, 1996.

Frost, H. *Crossing Stones*. New York: Frances Foster Books / Farrar, Straus, and Giroux, 2009.

Gerstein, M. *The Old Country*. New York: Roaring Brook Press, 2005.

Greenfield, E. *When the Horses Ride By: Children in the Times of War*. New York: Lee & Low, 2006.

Gregory, V. *When Stories Fell Like Shooting Stars*. New York: Simon & Schuster, 1996.

Hynes-Berry, M. *Don't Leave the Story in the Book*. New York: Teachers College Press, 2012.

Ingpen, R. *Peace Begins with You*. San Francisco: Sierra Club/Little, Brown, 1989.

Janks, H. "Critical Literacy: beyond reason" *Australian Educational Researcher,* Vol. 29 No. 1 7–27, 2002.

Johnson, E. & Vasudevan, L. "Seeing and Hearing Students' Lived and Embodied Critical Literacy Practices." *Theory into Practice*. Vol.51: 34–41, 2012.

Kohn, A. *No Contest: The Case Against Competition*. Boston, MA: Houghton Mifflin Co., 1986.

Kohn, A. *The Brighter Side of Human Nature: Altruism and Empathy in Everyday Life*. New York: Basic Books, 1990.

Kohn, A. *Beyond Discipline: From Compliance to Community*. Alexandria, VA: Association for Supervision and Curriculum Development, 1996.

Krinitz, E. N. & Steinhardt, B. *Memories of Survival*. New York: Hyperion, 2005.

Kuklin, S. *No Choirboy: Murder, Violence, and Teenagers on Death Row*. New York: Henry Holt, 2008.

Kurtz, E. & Ketchum, K. *The Spirituality of Imperfection: Modern Wisdom from Ancient Classics*. New York: Bantam Books, 1992.

Kuykendall, C. *From Rage to Hope: Strategies for Reclaiming Black and Hispanic Students*. Bloomington, IN: National Education Service, 1992.

Langton, J. *The Fragile Flag*. New York: Harper & Row, 1984.

Lantieri, L. & Patti, J. *Waging Peace in our Schools*. Boston, MA: Beacon Press, 1996.

Law, N. "Children and War." Position paper for the Association of Childhood Education International. February, 1973.

Levine, K. *Hana's Suitcase: A True Story*. Park Ridge, IL: Albert Whitman, 2003.

Lewis, B. A. *The Kid's Guide to Social Action*, revised edition. Minneapolis, MN: Free Spirit Publishing, 1998.

McKee, D. *The Conquerors*. Handprint Books, 2004.

Myers, W. D. *Monster*. New York: HarperCollins, 1999.

Naidoo, B. *Out of Bounds: Seven Stories of Conflict and Hope*. New York: HarperCollins, 2003.

Nivola, C.A. *Planting the Trees of Kenya: The Story of Wangari Maathai*. New York: Frances Foster Books / Farrar, Straus and Giroux, 2008.

Oppenheim, J. *Dear Miss Breed: True Stories of the Japanese Incarceration During World War II and a Librarian Who Made a Difference*. New York: Scholastic Nonfiction / Scholastic, 2006.

Paley, V. G. *The Girl with the Brown Crayon: How Children Use Stories to Shape their Lives*. Cambridge: Harvard University Press, 1997.

Partridge, E. *Marching for Freedom: Walk Together, Children, and Don't You Grow Weary*. New York: Viking, 2009.

Radunsky, V. *What Does Peace Feel Like?* New York: An Anne Schwartz Book / Atheneum, 2004.

Rodari, G. *The Grammar of Fantasy.* New York: Teachers and Writers Collaborative, 1996.

Rumford, J. *Silent Music: A Story of Bagdhad.* New York: A Neal Porter Book / Roaring Brook Press, 2008.

Russo, M. *Always Remember Me: How One Family Survived World War II.* New York: An Anne Schwartz Book / Atheneum, 2005.

Satrapi, M. *Persepolis: The Story of a Childhood.* New York: Pantheon, 2003.

Sepetys, R. *Between Shades of Gray.* New York: Philomel, 2011.

Skarmeta, A. *The Composition.* Madeira Park, BC, Canada: A Groundwood Book/ Douglas & McIntyre, 2000.

Smith, I. *Half Spoon of Rice: A Survival Story of the Cambodian Genocide.* Manhattan Beach, CA: East West Discovery Press, 2010.

Thomas, S. M. *Somewhere Today: A Book of Peace.* Park Ridge, IL: Albert Whitman, 1998.

Tonatiuh, D. *Separate Is Never Equal: Sylvia Mendez & Her Family's Fight for Desegregation.* New York: Abrams, 2014.

Weatherford, C. B. *Birmingham, 1963.* Honesdale, PA: Wordsong / Boyds Mills Press, 2007.

Williams, K. L. & Mohammed, K. *Four Feet, Two Sandals.* Grand Rapids, MI: Eerdmans, 2007.

Winter, J. *Nasreen's Secret School: A True Story from Afghanistan.* La Jolla, CA: Beach Lane, 2009.

Woodson, J. *Peace, Locomotion.* Westminster, London, UK: Putnam, 2009.

Zarambouka, S. *Irene-Peace: Includes a Play/Aristophanes.* Washington, D.C.: Tee Loftin, 1979.

Zipes. J. *Creative Storytelling: Building Community, Changing Lives.* New York: Routledge, 1995.

Zipes, J. *The Great Fairy Tale Tradition: From Straparola and Basile to the Brothers Grimm.* New York: Norton, 2001.

Zipes, J. *Fairy Tale as Myth/Myth as Fairy Tale.* Lexington: University Press of Kentucky, 1994.

Zipes, J. *Happily Ever After: Fairy Tales, Children, and the Culture Industry.* New York: Routledge, 1997.

Zipes, J. *Speaking Out: Storytelling and Creative Drama for Children.* New York: Routledge, 2004.

Zipes, J. *Why Fairy Tales Stick: The Evolution and Relevance of a Genre.* New York: Routledge, 2006.

Online Resources for Peace & Social Justice

Another Mother. http://anothermother.org/

Digital Activity Center. http://www2.peacefirst.org/digitalactivitycenter/resources/search

Dudding, K. *Americans All of Us.* http://www.americansallofus.com/

Montclair State University. "6 Elements of Social Justice Ed." http://6elementssje.blogspot.com

Education World. "Ten Social Justice Activities to Try in Class." http://www.educationworld.com/a_lesson/social-justice-activities-students.shtml

Edudemic. "6 Videos to Use in Your Social Justice Lessons." http://www.edudemic.com/6-videos-use-social-justice-lessons/

Edutopia. "Creating Classrooms for Social Justice." http://www.edutopia.org/blog/creating-classrooms-for-social-justice-tabitha-dellangelo

Lewis, C. & Ingram, D., et al. (2010) "Critical Literacy in Neighborhood Bridges: An Exploratory Study." *Center for Applied Research and Educational Improvement.* http://blog.lib.umn.edu/cehd/carei/

Lewis, C. *Literary Practices as Social Acts: Power Status, and Cultural Norms in the Classroom.* Mahwah, NJ: Lawrence Erlbaum, 2001.

Lewis, C. & Ingram, D., et al. "Making the Body Visible through Dramatic/Creative Play: Critical Literacy in Neighborhood Bridges." *Center for Applied Research and Educational Improvement.* http://blog.lib.umn.edu/cehd/carei/, 2010.

Museum of Tolerance. "Lessons and Activities." http://www.museumoftolerance.com/site/c.tmL6KfNVLtH/b.5063231/

Myrick, A.M. "Folktales and Philanthropy: Using Folktales as a Bridge to Community Service." *SIT Graduate Institute/SIT Study Abroad DigitalCollections@SIT* http://digitalcollections.sit.edu/cgi/viewcontent.cgi?article=1698&context=ipp_collection

NYSUT. "Speak Truth to Power: Human Rights Defenders who are Changing Our World." http://blogs.nysut.org/sttp/category/lesson-plans/

PBS Parents. "Children's Books about Peace." http://www.pbs.org/parents/ adventures-in-learning/2014/09/childrens-books-peace/

Peace Tales. http://www.peacetales.org/peace_tales.html

Teaching Tolerance. https://www.tolerance.org/classroom-resources/ tolerance-lessons/using-photographs-to-teach-social-justice

Using Their Words. http://www.usingtheirwords.org/childrens-literature/

Wolf, James ("Brother Wolf). *The Art of Storytelling* podcasts http://www. artofstorytellingshow.com/past-guests/

Interview #050 La'Ron Williams—"Supporting peace and social justice through storytelling."

Interview #088 Elisa Pearmain—"Teaching Forgiveness through storytelling."

Interview #070 Elizabeth Ellis— "Storytelling and the Development of Ethical Behavior."

World Organizations Strive to Establish Peace. https://listsurge. com/20-world-organizations-strive-establish-world-peace/

WONDER

Sources for Stories that Address Peace & Social Justice

Bedtime stories ... to wake up! Stories about peace. http://freestoriesforkids.com/ tales-for-kids/values-and-virtues/stories-about-peace

Chace, K. Teaching *Tolerance—Promoting Peace.* http://www.storybug.net/links/ peace.html

Durrell, A. & Sachs, M. (eds.) *The Big Book of Peace.* New York: Dutton, 1990.

Feldman, C. & Kornfield, J. *Stories of the Spirit, Stories of the Heart: Parables of the Spiritual Path from Around the World.* New York: HarperCollins, 1991.

Floating Eagle Feather (ed.) *... And the Earth Lived Happily Ever After: Old and New Traditional Tales to Wage Peace.* Metairie, LA: Wages of Peace, 1987.

Hines, A.G. *Peaceful pieces: poems and quilts about peace.* New York: Henry Holt, 2011.

"How Violence Ended," at *Author Online! Aaron Shepard's Home Page Stories, Scripts, and More.* http://www.aaronshep.com/stories/040.html

Johnston, T. *Voice from afar: poems of peace.* New York: Holiday House, 2008.

Katz, K. *Can You Say Peace?* New York: Square Fish Publishing, 2016.

Lobel, A. *Potatoes, Potatoes.* New York: Greenwillow, 2004.

MacDonald, M.R. "Grandfather Bear Is Hungry" in *Look Back and See: Lively Tales for Gentle Tellers*. New York: H.W. Wilson, 1991.

MacDonald, M. R. *Peace Tales: World Folktales to Talk About*. Hamden, CT: Linnet Books, 1992.

McCutcheon, J. *Christmas in the Trenches*. Atlanta: Peachtree Press, 2006.

Muth, J. J. *Stone Soup*. New York: Scholastic Press, 2003.

Hamanaka, S. *On the Wings of Peace: Writers and Illustrators Speak Out for Peace, in Memory of Hiroshima and Nagasaki*. New York: Clarion Books, 1995.

PeaceGarrett: Peace Stories for Children. https://peacegarret.wordpress.com/peace-stories-for-children/

Kids for Peace: Uplifting our World Through Love and Action. https://kidsforpeaceglobal.org/about/

Pearman, E. D. *Once Upon A Time—Storytelling to Teach Character and Prevent Bullying*. Greensboro, N.C.: Character Development Group, Inc., 2006.

"The Red and Blue Coat," in Forest, H. *Wisdom Tales from Around the World*. Little Rock, AR: August House, 1996.

Scholes, K. *Peace Begins with You*. San Francisco: Sierra Club Books, 1990.

Storytellers for World Change Network (compilers). *Weaving Words, Spinning Hope: A Collection of Stories and Teacher Activities to help Children Explore Issues of Peace, Justice and Social Awareness*. Philadelphia: New Society Press, 1991.

Thiele, B. & Weiss, G.D. *What a Wonderful World*. New York: Henry Holt & Co., 2014.

"The War for the Skies," in Pierce, M. & Jennings, K. *Storytelling Tips & Tales*. Glenview, IL: Goodyear Books, 1999.

If you have benefitted from this book, point your web browser to:

https://www.storytellerlynford.com

http://www.sherrynorfolk.com

www.storynet.org

https://www.parkhurstbrothers.com